1992

EDUCATION AND ETHNICITY:
THE U.S. EXPERIMENT IN SCHOOL INTEGRATION

by
Ralph Scott

Journal of Social, Political and Economic Studies
Monograph Series
Volume 17

The Council for Social and Economic Studies
Washington, D.C.

ISBN 0-930690-20-6

The Council for Social and Economic Studies
1133 13th Street, N.W., Suite C-2
Washington, D.C. 20005

Manufactured in the United States of America

CONTENTS

PREFACE

The United States of America is today a nation made up of many minorities, and its educational system is operating under critical difficulties. Courtland Milloy of the *Washington Post* recently asserted that "Never in history have there been so many black youths without an iota of job experience." A visit to virtually any U.S. desegregated school reveals that for far too many of the disadvantaged youths of all races, these schools have become the training ground for later unemployability.

It is perplexing that circumstances have worsened for literally millions of minority youths during a period which has witnessed the burgeoning of special programs designed to help them. The entire structure of U.S. education has been reshaped to implement race-conscious educational provisions. Forced busing ordered by courts to bring about a racial "balance" in the classrooms marked the first step in a process which has diverted schools from their historical emphasis on education to a new emphasis upon social engineering.

As U.S. schools become racially "balanced," educators are forced to deal with large ethnic achievement gaps at the high school level: the average reading and math scores for white students, for example, exceeds the average for blacks by as much as three grade levels. Recognizing that teachers cannot effectively deal with the wide achievement spread within classrooms, which appeared after busing, school administrators frequently employed a practice known as ability grouping to bring educational materials and assignments more into line with the abilities of individual students. But critics faulted ability grouping as 'resegregation,' and this charge was supported in the sense that disproportionately large numbers of blacks and Hispanics were placed on the lower tracks. Ability grouping was abolished, and classrooms and instructional groupings were racially balanced. Other race-conscious intervention measures followed: informal quotas on promotions, on participation in extra-curricular activities, and in the composition of special classrooms such as those for the gifted and mentally retarded.

A causal relationship exists between race-sensitive schooling policies and the worsening plight of many minority students. The destruction of neighborhood schools has weakened the essential bonds of home, school and community. Ethnic quotas on discipline and suspensions have forced teachers to tolerate behavior which is most efficaciously curbed during the formative years. Unrealistic grading policies have led a large fraction of students to look with disdain upon unskilled jobs which offer opportunities for gainful employment. Uncritical promotions, ignoring students' actual academic competencies, have led to unacceptably high failure rates in high school and universities and even to the certification of unqualified professionals, as verified by the high failure rates of blacks on teacher competency tests. In short, race-conscious schooling practices have directly contributed to the 'nightmarish' problems of specific minorities in the U.S. about which Milloy has so eloquently written. Black and other minority parents must work to see that schools veer back on course, and emphasize learning and instruction rather than race quotas and other politically motivated goals.

INTRODUCTION
LAW AND THE SOCIAL SCIENCES: THE U.S. EXPERIMENT IN ENFORCED SCHOOL INTEGRATION

Concerned about the widely disparate performance of different ethnic groups in school classrooms, the United States embarked upon a system of legally-enforced school integration based upon theories advanced by certain social scientists that minority children would perform better if attending class in the company of white American children.

For the past quarter century, the racial 'desegregation' of schools has been one of the most significant, and unresolved, social issues in the U.S. Every president since Eisenhower has identified busing as the uppermost of contemporary schooling questions, and Derrick Bell (1973, p. 460) has observed that *Brown* (1954), the Supreme Court ruling which set desegregation into motion, has "fathered a social upheaval, the extent and consequences of which cannot even now be measured with certainty. It marks a divide in American life." This paper discusses some of the legal, political, and social science dynamics played out at *Brown*; associates invalidity of social science testimony presented in that landmark case with professional bias and ideological imbalance; examines the relevance of *Brown* to current judicial rulings on desegregation; proposes that the courts at least tacitly recognize problems which have stemmed from not hearing both sides of the complex issue; urges academia to enhance the quality of judicial proceedings through concerted efforts to reduce ideological contamination; and, finally, suggests that the most feasible way for social science to contribute to educational equity lies in a maximization of objectivity through reform within the various professional disciplines and through use of new appraisal techniques such as micro-data analysis.

Can Social Science Enhance Judicial Rulings on Sensitive Subjects?

There are those who hope that social science will play a leading role in creating improved understandings of desegregation. In a treatise on busing effects, Levin and Moise (1975, p. 133) argue that a new union of law and social science is required because the determination of harm and the specifications of remedy are so complex the courts must work from a "more solid foundation of fact than ever before in deciding questions of law ... It is legal development which places increasing importance on the research of social scientists." Taylor

(1978, p. 71) offers a different view, and asserts that wide-spread doubts exist in the scientific, legal and political communities as to the objectivity, maturity and relevance of the social sciences to the constitutional decisions rendered by the courts. This, he says, is in part attributable to what are perceived as the failures of the social scientific-based political strategies during the War on Poverty of the 1960s.

Despite uncertainty within both the legal and the social science camps, an emerging interdisciplinary liaison has proceeded well beyond the flirtation stage. Initially, and as might have been expected, events augured well for the new union. In *Brown*, the Court cast caution aside and relied heavily on social science for a key conclusion: segregated schools generate feelings of inferiority which contribute to a tendency to retard the educational and mental development of Negro children, thus depriving them of (educational, emotional, and social) benefits they would receive in a racially integrated school system (*Brown*, 1954; Wilkinson, 1979, p. 32). But, as Bickel (1973, pp. 100-101) — law clerk of Justice Frankfurter during *Brown* — notes, it was here that the Court may have made its first wrong turn. In outlawing *de jure* segregation, the Court indicated that education cannot be successful unless children of all groups are taught together. This caused the distinction between *de jure* and *de facto* segregation to blur. One consequence of *Brown*, therefore, has been for the courts not only to render illegal the exclusion of students from attending neighborhood schools on the basis of race, but to frequently bring about precisely the opposite — forcing children to attend distant schools — by ordering racial balance for purposes of providing equal opportunity.

Unquestioned in the current debate concerning busing effects on educational equity is the right of students to attend neighborhood schools, irrespective of race. That aspect of *Brown* commands near-unanimous approval. The real issue is whether all children should be able to attend neighborhood schools on a color-blind basis, or if racial balance is an imperative to quality education and the realization of constitutional requirements. Generally, judges have assumed that educational benefits will follow racial balance, and their rulings have therefore mirrored what has been considered consistent with a realistic remedy: racial balance. Significantly, judges experienced in desegregation matters have frequently appeared unaware of the diverse views social scientists hold as to what is required to enhance learning of vulnerable and poor children. Judge Julius Chambers (1977, p. 43), for example, claims that "social scientists agree that desegregated educational opportunities have resulted in substantial improvement of minority students." In Florida, Judge George Carr (Scott, 1981, p. 25) ruled that only when black freshmen have had the educational benefits of a totally desegregated school may literacy tests be implemented. A major contention of this paper is that the desegregation-achievement thesis cannot be validated and if minority students are to gain an opportunity for better schooling then busing must be abandoned, and viable educational measures substituted.

Initial Test for Social Science: *Brown*

To a substantial extent, judicial oversimplication of the complex processes involved in human learning can be traced to *Brown*, wherein the Court resolved separate desegregatory rulings from Delaware, Kansas, South Carolina, Virginia, and Washington, D.C. In these preliminary cases, little testimony was offered to counter the pro-desegregation testimony of NAACP social scientists. In preparing for the South Carolina case, the NAACP had ample opportunity to sense general academic uncertainty as to just what might be the educational consequences of school desegregation.* The NAACP encountered unexpected difficulty in lining up its witnesses. William H. Kilpatrick, considered the most impressive and effective professional educator of the period, felt that the NAACP case would "put back the long-run cause" (Kluger, p. 335). Elsa Robinson, a respected psychologist at New York University's Graduate School of Arts and Sciences, said "There is as yet no scientifically verifiable material of an empirical nature which bears directly on the issue" (Kluger, p. 336). Professors Gordon Allport and Joseph Rhine also declined to testify. But both

---

* Unlike the NAACP, the U.S. Supreme Court appeared unaware that some academicians doubted the value of desegregation and the NAACP's Thurgood Marshall did not assist the Court in gaining a better perspective. Asked by Justice Frankfurter if it would make any difference if the record contained the testimony of six professors who gave contrary testimony from that of the NAACP experts, Marshall replied: "I do not believe that there are any experts in the country who would so testify ... I know of no scientist that has made any study whether he be anthropologist or sociologist, who does not admit that segregation harms the child."

men suggested Otto Klineberg who had done research on the relationship between black migration to the North and IQ changes (Kluger, p. 336). A brief review of Klineberg's research illustrates the extent to which the Supreme Court, during *Brown*, appears to have uncritically accepted spurious claims.

Nothing in Klineberg's research spoke directly to the question of desegregatory effects within schools (Scott, 1966; Scott, 1975, pp. 97-106). In his most fundamental study, Klineberg had asked four of his graduate students to compare test scores of black migrants to New York City with those of resident blacks. It was predicted that the (segregated) new arrivals from the South would obtain lower scores than the (integrated) blacks who had lived in the North.

Results were not exactly as Klineberg had predicted. Except for a few blacks who had been in New York seven to eight years, the first student (Traver) found test scores unrelated to length of residence. Similar results were reported by Marks, a second student. The two remaining students, Yates and Lapidus, did remarkably better. They both reported that, on average, the newly arrived blacks were mentally retarded while blacks who had resided in New York eleven years scored within the low average range of intelligence. These remarkable data went unchallenged. Klineberg's studies contained additional shortcomings. The data were cross-sectional, the test used (*National Intelligence Test*) lacked validity and reliability. Overall, the experiment would fail to qualify for any but an ideologically-based professional journal. However, the results were included in the now famous Footnote 11, and contributed to the Court's ultimate conclusions.

Other contributors to Footnote 11 hardly advanced the ultimate credibility of social science. Perhaps the most telling testimony was that of Kenneth Clark, former president of the American Psychological Association who was lauded in *Psychology Today*: "Among the national leaders (of *Brown*) alive today, Dr. Kenneth Clark has no peer in scholarly or applied knowledge of ghetto psychology, or of educational and employment inequities in every sector of our society. The 1954 U.S. Supreme Court decisions on school desegregation were based in large part on an appendix to the legal briefs. This appendix came from a study, headed by Clark, on the tragedy of segregated education. The poverty approach of the Office of Economic Opportunity has been based on the two-year study

produced in 1964 by Harlem Youth Opportunities Unlimited
under his direction. He has received as many honors for his
work as any man in public affairs ..." (Hall, 1968) Clark's
testimony has been hailed within academia, but also soundly
criticized (Kluger, op cit. pp. 355-56; Scott, 1975, pp. 143-150)
in a manner consistent with Clark's own admission to NAACP
attorneys that it was impossible to isolate the effect of school
segregation as a factor in psychological damage Negro children
suffer. (Kluger, p. 353) Nonetheless, he testified that school
segregation definitely harmed black children. Richard Funston
(1977, p. 36) asserts that "Clark's famous 'doll test' involved a
hucksterish sleight of hand, and anyone who has ever examined
Gunnar Myrdal's *An American Dilemma* can only conclude
it is about as scientific as a seed catalogue."

Even as *Brown* was argued, and within the NAACP's inner
circle, misgivings arose concerning the unfolding social science
strategy. Columbia law professor Jack B. Weinstein was particularly unimpressed: "I may have used the word 'crap' to describe
the doll tests, which I'm afraid upset Kenneth (Clark) ... I
thought it absurd to try to couch our argument in terms of
dubious psychological data. I didn't want us to build our case
on a gimmick." (Kluger, op. cit., p. 355-56) In 1975, the same
Weinstein, then a federal judge, dealt with a challenge to the
very (*Brown*) data he had questioned in the 1950s. Asked to
rule if blacks may have the right to choose neighborhood
schools, even if they are segregated, in view of evidence presented in a then-recent social science review (Mosteller and
Moynihan, 1972), Weinstein replied "This position would have
to be rejected even were there basis in fact for the proposition
that segregated schools improved the education of black students — a proposition belied by data to date" (*Hart v. Community School Board*, 1975, Levin and Moise, op. cit., p. 91).

The most plausible explanation for the poor quality of social
science made available to the high court, and acceptance of
highly doubtful evidence by the nation's presumably most
august body, is that the times were not amenable to a dis-
passionate treatment of so emotional a topic as desegregation:
A fear barrier was erected, which inhibited social scientists
from dispassionately examining desegregation outcomes.
Certainly the NAACP made the best of the fact that the Court
was asked to render a decision not only of largely emotional
content but also of international significance. Said James

Nabrit, a Howard law professor and NAACP advisor: "Let the
Supreme Court take the blame if it dares say to the entire
world 'Yes, democracy rests on a legalized caste system. Segregation of races is legal.' Make the court choose ..." (Kluger,
p. 537)

Significantly, *Brown* was argued at a time when academia
was dealing with an active McCarthyism. More than a few
professors were ready to become involved in activism. David
Kretch fell into this category. When the NAACP approached
the 42 year old psychologist, he volunteered that he was "more
than eager to strike a blow for Truth and Beauty" [as, says
Kluger (pp. 337-38), "Truth and Beauty were perceived in
those more innocent times."] Indeed, *Brown* hearings were
conducted as professional reaction to McCarthysim, and perceived dangers of "conservatives" to academic integrity, neared
a zenith. When Kenneth Clark remarked that "the entire atmo-
sphere of New York City College was heady, and every scholar
was eager to relate classroom work to social action," (Kluger,
p. 130) he could have been describing conditions at dozens
of American Universities.

As the NAACP pressed the case, its vulnerable social science
testimony received welcome buffering. Louisiana State University professor Peter A. Carmichael (1973) observes that defense
attorneys were refused opportunity to cross-examine NAACP
experts. The rigor of the *Brown* testimony was further reduced
by discrimination within professional circles. In three related
trials prior to *Brown*, none of the opposition produced witnesses
who disputed NAACP claims, and NAACP opponents were
initially surprised at the difficulty they experienced in finding
academics willing to testify for them. They soon discovered
why. Archibald R. Robertson, representing Virginia, unsuccessfully talked to more than 100 prospective witnesses. Most of
them said that their views would likely prove so unpopular
among their colleagues that it might well ruin their careers
to testify. (Kluger pp. 482, 545) There was one exception.

George Modlin, President of the University of Richmond,
suggested Henry Garrett of Columbia University, a past president of the American Psychological Association. Garrett was
willing to testify. But when word of this reached the dean of
graduate faculties at Columbia, Garrett was told that the
university dealt with "a pretty explosive situation" in its
relationship with the surrounding Harlem community, and that

his testifying in Virginia might embarrass Columbia. Garrett later detailed the repeated infringement on his academic freedom which resulted from his act of testifying. (Kluger, pp. 483-84) Except for Garrett, no prominent social scientist cautioned the Court on the uncertain consequences, for children, of desegregation. The stage was set for the justices — however divided on other matters — to unanimously conclude that black children would, academically and emotionally, derive benefit from attending school with white children.

The Consequences of *Brown*

Subsequent to the high court's ruling, lower federal courts were inclined to uncritically assume segregatory harm, assess desegregatory remedy and then supervise the "integration" process. More often than not, the governing factor at trial turned out to be the personal leanings of the federal district judge (Wilkenson, p. 80). On the lower court levels it was generally assumed, as Kenneth Clark noted, that *Brown* affirmed that segregated schools alone were responsible for the academic inequities witnessed with so many black students. In *Hobson vs. Hansen* (1967), Judge J. Skelly Wright reflected judicial naivete, so common more than a decade after *Brown*: "Racially and socially homogeneous schools damage the minds and spirits of all children ... The scholastic achievement of the disadvantaged child, Negro and White, is strongly related to the racial and socio-economic composition of the student body ... A racially and socially integrated school environment increases the scholastic achievement of the disadvantaged child of whatever race ... Placing the child in lower tracks for reduced education based on (inappropriate) tests, thus implementing the self-fulfilling prophecy phenomenon inherent in such misjudgment, inferior teachers, textbooks unrelated to the lives of the disadvantaged children, inadequate remedial programs — all have contributed to the increase in crime, particularly juvenile crime." Not a single one of these assertions can, even today, be empirically validated.

Having access to only one side of the busing argument, judges issued orders which could only confuse and anger parents, minority and majority alike. In Grand Rapids, Michigan, one judge ruled in favor of various school practices which, in nearby Kalamazoo, another judge declared unconstitutional.

The Sixth Circuit Court of Appeals affirmed both judgments. (Wilkinson, 1979, p. 200).

Given the historical circumstances, it can be understood why judges considered desegregation an appropriate remedy, even when this meant racial balancing, or the dismantling of neighborhood schools. Rarely, if ever, was conventional desegregatory wisdom questioned during judicial hearings. And on those infrequent occasions when scholars presented evidence that busing might not enhance learning they were sometimes subjected to attacks from the bench. In one lower court decision, significance was given to Thomas Pettigrew's (empirically unverified) claim that a certain percentage of minority students was required for successful integration: the opposing expert testimony of Professor Hooker was rejected as racist, even though it had the approval of CORE. (Bell, p. 518)

The Coleman Report: Orthodoxy Challenged

For more than a decade after *Brown*, the "busing-benefit" thesis was rarely challenged by social scientists who have demonstrated, in practically any other subject, a remarkable capacity to openly disagree. In 1966, however, *Equality of Educational Opportunity* (Coleman, 1966) was released. This federally-funded research project drew data from approximately 645,000 students and 60,000 teachers; the study became popularly known as the *Coleman Report*. Throughout governmental and professional circles, it was confidently expected that the *Coleman Report* would conclude that schools for minority students would have fewer resources, poorer educational programs, and fewer qualified teachers. The minority-majority achievement gap, it was assumed, could therefore be traced to "inferior" schools. This, in turn, would strengthen the case for integration since money presumably flowed into schools attended by whites.

Coleman's findings, however, failed to affirm the popular and conventional assumptions. For the first time, official doubt arose concerning the social science upon which *Brown* had been built. The *Report* revealed that, when family background factors were controlled, differences between schools accounted for only a small fraction of differences in pupil achievement. Writing in *Science*, Robert C. Nichols (1966) remarked "The findings (of the *Coleman Report*) are too astonishing to be accepted." Coleman quickly came under attack, and initially sought to render his data more acceptable by claiming that black children learned more effectively when they attended schools with a majority of (middle class) whites. (Coleman, 1968) But on this he was quickly challenged. Henry S. Dyer (1968) of the Educational Testing Services observed "There is nothing whatsoever in the Coleman analysis that can justify such an inference. The Coleman study contains no data at all on the effects that might accrue from putting minority pupils with different kinds of classmates."

Since publication of the 1966 study, Coleman (1979, 1981) has proceeded to conduct, and report, subsequent research which counterindicates educational or social gains associated with desegregation. His reports have not set well with long-time busing advocates, whose responses provide insight into the reluctance of social scientists to report findings inconsistent with the "busing-benefit" equation. Kenneth Clark urged social scientists to chastise Coleman. In a statement that belies awareness of just how uncritically his *Brown* testimony was received both within law and social science, Clark complained that pro-busing advocates like himself "are more likely to be required to meet the most severe tests of scientific integrity and personal probity." (Rist and Anson, p. 5) Nathanial Jones, former NAACP General Counsel and now a federal judge, declared: "Dr. James Coleman is a fraud ... thoroughly repudiated by his colleagues" (Rist and Anson, p. 119) Coleman, once regarded in federal circles as the top authority on desegregatory effects, has responded that Clark is blind to uncomfortable data and is unable to understand where his own advocacy led. (Wilkinson, p. 180).

In recent years, claims of educational benefits related to desegregation have come under closer scrutiny, and considerable doubts have arisen on matters once considered closed. Harold Howe (1972), former U.S. Commissioner for Education, has conceded that "the lively research of statistically-oriented social scientists casts some shadows on conventional assumptions about the benefits of integration, particularly in the schools." Throughout the 1970s and into the 1980s, the fear barrier to identifying counterproductive consequences of busing has been increasingly breached. A steady series of publications, while still representing a minority perspective within academia, has provided statistical support for the positions that desegregation (1) promotes resegregation, leaving public schools to serve poor and minority children, as a result of white or middle-class flight (Scott, 1979: Armor, 1981)(2) does not enhance minority learning (Wilson, 1979; Gerard and Miller, 1976; Scott, 1981); and (3) fails to promote racial harmony (Maruyama and Miller, 1979; Fisher, 1981). Separately, on the twenty-fifth anniversary of *Brown*, the U.S. Department of Health Education and Welfare readied a special issue (*Prejudice and Pride*, 1979), designed to hail gains achieved through the high court's decision. Unexpectedly, the select panel of experts disagreed concerning busing outcomes. Some thought *Brown* had caused social and educational problems. HEW refused to release the report in time for the *Brown* observances.

Perhaps nowhere were conflicting signals on busing objectives more apparent than within the NAACP itself. The organization — which during *Brown* had wired its major financial contributors that "opportunities for decent public education" of black children depended upon the outcome of *Brown* (Kluger, p. 617) — now objects to the introduction of evidence that busing impedes black learning. (Wolf, 1977, p. 116; 1981, p. 226).

The Judiciary Reassesses Social Science Contributions

Accumulation of discouraging statistics on desegregatory effects has prompted judges to reassess their views. In so doing, as noted by J. Harvie Wilkinson (1979, p. 190) professor of constitutional law at the University of Virginia, there has been growing judicial distrust of academia. More than a few judges have come to believe that casual acceptance of doubtful social science has contributed to a drop of public confidence in the courts. With issues such as desegregation in mind, Chief Justice Warren Burger declared that "The American people are nearing an end of their patience with the American machinery of justice." (Stein, p. 1) Some judges have opted to disassociate their rulings with social science, and to link decisions not with (measurable) schooling benefits but with (more abstruse) constitutional guarantees. Judge J. Skelly Wright, whose decisions for years were laced with social science assumptions, declared "a plague on the house of social science." Judge William E. Doyle (1977a, 1977b) minimized the significance of social science presented at *Brown* and claimed that school desegregation rulings are not based on social science evidence. Rather, he said, such decisions are "founded on much more fundamental precepts — organic, moral, positive law and reason."

The ordinary layman (and considerably more people) may have difficulty following an increasingly popular judicial line: on the one hand it is claimed that *Brown* determined that segregated schooling was harmful and the issue is therefore no longer open for study, although practically all desegregatory research has been conducted since *Brown.* Conversely, it is also held that social science — far more sophisticated than that contained in Footnote 11 — is irrelevant. Judge John Minor Wisdom belongs to this new school of judicial thought. "Social science research appears to have no effect on the most important busing decisions of the 1970s," says Wisdom. (Wilkinson, p. 190) However, for years Judge Wisdom ardently supported pro-desegregatory testimony, while rejecting any academic challenge to the then prevailing theory of "busing benefits." An illustration: In *Evers vs. Jackson Municipal School District* (1964), District Judge Mize permitted evidence to be introduced to show that separate schools were not injurious but instead advantageous to pupils of both races. Judge Mize expressed the view that this evidence "cries out for a reappraisal and complete reconsideration of the findings and conclusions of the United States Supreme Court in the *Brown* decision"; nonetheless, Mize granted the plaintiffs' injunction request, feeling bound by the prior Fifth Circuit holding in *Stell v. Savannah-Chatham County Board of Education.* Judge Wisdom, ruling for the Fifth Circuit on Appeal, declared that "these cases tax the patience of the court." (*Evers,* Cert. denied, 1966) In firmly rejecting an attempt "to overturn *Brown* on a factual showing," Wisdom declared that the inherent inequality of segregated schools was now a legal principle no longer open to question. However, this appears to carry the subtle racist assumption that black schools are inferior because they are attended by blacks.

As witnessed in *Evers,* there has been a general tendency for lower courts to maintain the principle that the harm of segregated schools is now a matter of law. (Wolf, 1977, 1981) Yet on this there has been some indecision. In *Bradley* (1972), Judge Roth permitted suburban school boards to take the deposition of David Armor who had written that "busing is not an effective policy instrument for raising the achievement of black students or for increasing interracial harmony." Later, Judge Roth refused to receive Armor's evidence in testimony on the grounds that it was irrelevant and represented "a new rationale for a return to the discredited 'separate but equal' policy." The issue was carried to the Sixth Circuit Court of Appeals where a majority sustained Judge Roth's ruling. In a dissenting opinion, (*Bradley v. Milliken, 6th* Circuit, 1977) Judge Weick concluded that sociological opinions and evidence should have been admitted because the high court had rested the *Brown* decision on sociological opinions.

Must "Absolutes" Collide?

The decision of the Warren Court to have argued the case against desegregation in terms of educational quality or anticipated achievement profiles was probably an error which has invited the collision of what Funston (1977) has considered "absolute" principles — which have a way of colliding with other "absolutes." An "absolute" says Funston, is likely, sooner or later, to collapse under its own weight and that is now what we currently witness. On desegregatory issues, it appears that four interrelated "absolutes" have slowly moved forward on a collision course: (1) The *Brown* decision, set in a moral context, with reliance on questionable social data which lower courts have declared closed to further inquiry; (2) actual consequences of racial balancing as documented by research conducted since the high court's ruling; (3) decline of public confidence in the public schools and in the judiciary and (4) social science and governmental leadership seemingly determined to advance desegregation irrespective of results. If these "absolutes" collide, the damage to society will hardly be inconsequential.

As yet, the "absolutes" have not directly collided. There is still time for reconsideration and policy shifts. Two of the absolutes — actual consequences of busing, and a decline in public confidence stemming from counterproductive educational policies based not on law and reason but on ideology — seem unchangeable. The remaining two "absolutes," however, may be malleable and hence not "absolutes": law and social science can learn to more objectively assess busing consequences and shape policies consistent with law and empirically cohesive research. There is little value, however, in failing to recognize the enormity of the task: conscious ego processes are unlikely to be decisive on emotionally charged issues (Koestler, 1967; Murphy, 1975; Schachtel, 1959). Yet the obvious need to provide poor and minority children with improved educational opportunities, coupled with growing awareness of the magnitude of problems faced within schools — may provide a sufficient drive for objectification of sensitive social issues such as busing.

The Supreme Court has yet to formally rule whether the evidence submitted at *Brown* is a matter of fact or of law. There is, therefore, still a possibility that the actual consequences of racial balancing may be reviewed with emphasis on remedies which enhance lifelong prospects of vulnerable youth. If, as many believe, *Brown* ruled only that children have the right to attend neighborhood schools, irrespective of race, and where violations have occured that effective remedies are to be ordered, then an escape hatch exists, through which opportunities for remedial reconsiderations, and use of validated social science, may flow. Many black leaders are calling for just that.

Tony Brown, executive producer of the *Black Journal*, claims that "there is a significant but silent Black majority view on busing that is virtually never heard. Because Black leaders are the only members of the Black community who get media exposure, the public hears only their perceptions of busing for integration purposes, and Black leaders are overwhelmingly in favor of busing." (Brown, 1977; Grassley, 1977). Brown has also called for a more rational approach to desegregation: "... Whites who oppose busing must lose their fear of being called racists and Blacks must stop the automatic adoption of integration as a cure-all for the problems of Black children. Both must embrace a higher principle of truth: It is not necessarily good or bad because it is Black or White. It is good or bad because it does or does not work." (Brown, 1977; Grassley, 1977) Black parents seem to agree: after experiencing not the rhetoric but the reality of having their children bused, black support for the practice decreases (Wilkinson, p. 245).

Perhaps the most recalcitrant of the "absolutes" involves objectivity within social science. Some who have studied academic bias in favor of social change have concluded that social science simply cannot put its house in order. One observor (Green, 1971) proposes that researchers deny their services to the existing power structure in order to support counter-vailing forces whose viewpoints are chronically underrepre-sented. His is not an isolated voice.

Fully four years after the appearance of the Coleman Report, Julian Stanley (1970), former president of the Division of Educational Psychology within the American Psychological Association, asserted that most measurement specialists know about false claims (such as unverified busing benefits) but are afraid to speak out while those who do speak up are likely to be labeled 'racists' or, at least, 'illiberal.' In her Carnegie-sponsored study of 60,000 faculty members, Carol Weiss (1977, p.8) found the overwhelming majority of social scientists to favor promoting social change such as busing. It is no exag-geration to say that influential organizations have not infre-quently advanced the careers of individuals not on the basis of demonstrable skills but for their loyalty to an ideology. The National Education Association and Phi Delta Kappa have elected to ignore data which indicate that busing is coun-terproductive, and instead have not only strongly supported busing, but have authorized publications which slyly hint at dark motives among educators who oppose busing. (Blanken-ship, 1969; Austin and Lecke, 1973; Phi Delta Kappa Editorial, 1975)

Separately, and in the fall of 1981, the U.S. Senate Sub-committee on Separation of Powers invited four experts to testify concerning achievement consequences of busing. The resulting debate revealed persuasive interpretations on both sides, but the setting did not provide either side opportunity for a clearly decisive victory. The author cannot claim an objective detachment from this issue, since he had just pre-sented a case against the desegregation-achievement thesis. (Scott, 1981b) Yet he was surprised to hear the Senate Sub-committee told that achievements of minority children in the Nashville-Davidson County (Tennessee) Schools had risen because of desegregation. Only two weeks before the Senate testimony was given, Tennessee NAACP leaders had charged that those very schools presently serve only black and poor children. (Finn, 1981) And four months before the hearings, Thomas Caulkins, Director of Assessment for Nashville-David-son County Schools, told the author there was no evidence of achievement benefits associated with desegregation.

The academic community was not given an objective report

of the congressional hearings. One influential journal, funded by the U.S. Department of Education and the National Institute of Education, responsible for the sub-funding of over a dozen Research and Development Centers, featured the Senate testimony in its quarterly publication. (Schneider, 1981) The resulting article oversimplified the complex desegregation issues. Entitled "School Integration Works for Kids," the article contained such statements as "My emotions joined with my common sense to tell me that the "pro-integration" crowd had a better argument ... My liberal beliefs intact, I leaned back (to hear an expert claim) 'All the best studies confirm the positive impact of desegregation on student achievement'..." Not considering himself a member of an "anti-integration crowd," this experimenter wrote to the organization which publishes the journal, asking if an article might be published which presented the "other side." The request was politely but firmly rejected. Almost a decade ago, in concluding their book *On Equality of Educational Opportunity*, Mosteller and Moynihan (1972) called for new, more objective, more balanced and more open attitudes toward research on desegregation. There is little tangible evidence that their call has yet been heeded in centers which significantly shape social science thought.

There is, however, reason to hope that fresh collaborative efforts between law and social science can win credibility and result in more effective schooling. Few observers dispute the critical need for major improvements in the learning climates and conditions provided minority and poor American youth. Prospective remedies will require rational and creative formulations, worthy of the best efforts of those who represent law and academia, and deliberately fashioned to reduce researcher bias.

Future Prospects for Interdisciplinary Efforts

Summing up, the complexity of issues such as school desegregation appears to require meaningful and responsible collaboration between law and social science. Effective intervention is not easy to accomplish, and law alone is insufficient if viable remedies are the desired goal. And yet, as the history of desegregatory law reveals,. past interdisciplinary efforts have failed to provide useful products: busing remedies have not been shown to "remedy." There is no evidence that schooling quality for minority or poor children has advanced an inch since *Brown.*

In one of his last published works, Bickel — (1973, p. 106) who witnessed the unfolding of *Brown* — noted that it is unrealistic to expect the courts, which to their present regret prematurely embraced social science, to now eat their words and renege on their decisions. But Bickel held out hope for future contributions to law from social science. Demonstrate to the courts, he said, that social science holds the potential of providing useful insights, that school districts are embarked on concerted long-range efforts of educational reform using sound social science techniques. Then without the need to renege on prior decisions and without any impairment of the general function of judicial review, courts can say that they now confront a new reality, which no longer requires old remedies.

Conceivably, interdisciplinary rapprochement of the quality Bickel suggested may be gained. But only if representatives of law and social science concentrate on methods to objectify and to grant a greater measure of tolerance within their crafts. Genuine debate on complex emotional issues must be encouraged and the misuse of academic power reduced if not eliminated. Eventually, academia must recognize that "McCarthyism" and "McCarthyism in reverse" possess the same characteristics and ultimately elicit the same consequences. To again quote Funston: "absolute" principles have a way of colliding with other "absolutes," and there is little place for ideological bias if durable collaboration of law and social science is to be realized.

Finally, statistical methods must be identified and employed which not only reduce the latitude for investigator bias, but involve readers in participatory efforts to understand actual effects of specific "remedies" on the lives of students, families, schools and communities. Micro-data analysis, which emphasizes actual statistics rather than ideology, is one technique which may prove to be a useful vehicle in the restoration of a credible liaison between law and social science, which in turn can contribute to the building of viable intervention remedies for disadvantaged and minority youth.

REFERENCES

Anderson, Louis V.
   1966   The effect of desegregation on the achievement and person-
           ality patterns of Negro children. Unpublished doctoral dis-
           sertation, George Peabody College for Teachers University
           Microfilm, Nashville, Tennessee, 66-11, 237.

Armor, David J.
   1981   On school busing and the 14th amendment. Hearings before
           the Constitutional Subcommittee of the U.S. Senate Judiciary
           Committee, May 14.

Austin, C. Danford and John Leeke
   1973   Education and Racism. Washington, D.C.: National Education
           Association.

Bell, Derrick A. Jr.
   1973   Race, racism and American law. Boston: Little, Brown & Co.

Bickel, Alexander.
   1973   Frontiers of school law. Topeka, Kansas: National Organiza-
           tion on Legal Problems of Education.

Blankenburg, Richard
   1969   A racist proposal. *Phi Delta Kappan*, Vol. L (5), January,
           p. 312.

Bradley, Laurence A. and Gifford W. Bradley
   1977   The academic achievement of black students in desegregated
           schools: A critical review. *Review of Education Research*,
           Vol. 47 (3), 1977, pp. 399-449.

Bradley v. Milliken
   1972   345 F. Suppl. 914, 921 (E.D. Mich.).
   1973   484 F. 2d, 215, 265 (6th Cir., 1973).

Brown v. Board of Educ.
   1954   347 U.S. 483,493.

Brown, Tony
   1977   Does busing work? WNET-TV, New York, March 13. Also:
           Grassley, Charles E. Forced busing does not work. *Congres-
           sional Record*, May, 13, 1977, E2992.

Bumstead, Richard
   1968   Hartford finds integration works. *Educate*, November, pp.
           25-35. It works — Project Concern. One of a series of
           successful compensatory education programs.

Carmichael, Peter A.
   1973   As cited in Carter, John D. The Warren Court and the Consti-
           tution. Louisiana: Gretna Pelican Publishing Co.

Chambers, Julius L.
   1977   Implementing the promise of *Brown*: Social science and the
           courts in future school litigation. In Rist, Ray C. and Anson,
           Ronald J. (Eds.) Education, social science and judicial process.
           New York: Columbian Teachers College Press.

Clark, Kenneth
   1973   Social policy, power and social science research, *Harvard
            Educational Review,* February, Vol. 43 (1), pp. 113-121.
            This article conveys rather explicit threats to academicians
            who disagree with Clark, who suggests that some social scien-
            tists (the context of Clark's remarks indicate these include
            James S. Coleman and Arthur Jencks, author of Inequality:
            A Reassessment of the effect of family and schooling in
            America. New York: Basic Books, 1972) are willing to "com-
            promise the fundamental humanity of dark skinned children
            and (who) by so doing provide public officials with rationaliza-
            tions for regressive policies of malignant neglect ... (thus
            becoming) agents of injustice. This role raises the serious
            question of whether social scientists and the type of research
            for which they are responsible should be permitted to have
            any direct role in decisions on important matters of equity,
            justice and equality of groups of human beings. Social scien-
            tists must set up an apparatus to monitor scrupulously their
            own work and involvement in matters affecting social policy.
            They must assume the responsibility for protecting a gullible
            public from the seductive pretentions of scientific infal-
            libility which are now increasingly being offered. Social
            scientists must assume the difficult role of monitoring with
            vigilance the partnership of regressive politicians and social
            scientists."
Coleman, James S., et al.
   1966   Equality of educational opportunity. Washington, D.C.:
            U.S. Government Printing Office.
Coleman, James S.
   1968   The concept of equality of educational opportunity. In
            Miller, L.P. and E.W. Gordon (Eds), Equality of educational
            opportunity. New York: AMS Press, 1974 (reprinted from
            Harvard Educational Review Vol. 38, 1968, pp. 7-22.)
   1979   As cited in Prejudice and pride: The Brown decision after
            twenty-five years. U.S. Department of Health, Education and
            Welfare, pp. 14-15.
   1981   As cited in *Time,* April 20, p. 50.
Crain, Robert L. and Rita E. Mahard
   1978   Desegregation and black achievement: A review of the re-
            search. *Law and Contemporary Problems,* Vol. 42 (3), Sum-
            mer, 1978, pp. 17-56. (A preliminary report, containing
            essentially the same information, appeared in 1977 and was
            published by the National Review Panel on School Desegrega-
            tion Research, Institute on Policy Studies and Public Affairs,
            Duke University, Durham, North Carolina.)
Doyle, William E.
   1977 (a) Social science evidence in court cases. *Educational Forum*
            Vol. 41, March, pp. 263-270 (Also pp. 11-19 in Rist and
            Anson, op. cit.).
   1977 (b) Social science evidence in court cases. In Rist, Ray C. and

Ronald J. Anson, (Eds), Education, social science and the judicial process. New York: Columbia Teachers College Press, pp. 11-17.

Dyer, Henry S.
1968   School factors and equal educational opportunity. *Harvard Educational Review*, Vol. 38, Winter, p. 53.

Evans, Charles Lee
1969   The immediate effects of classroom integration on the academic progress, self-concept and racial attitudes of Negro elementary children. Unpublished doctoral dissertation, North Texas State University, Denton, Texas.
1971   Short term desegregation effects: The academic achievement of bused students. Fort Worth Independent School District, Fort Worth, Texas, 1972 (ERIC Document Reproduction Service No. ED 086 759).
1972-73 Integration evaluation: Desegregation Study II — academic effects on bused black and white students. Fort Worth Independent School District, Fort Worth, Texas, 1973.

Evers v. Jackson Municipal Separate School District
1964   232 F. Suppl. 241 (S.D. Miss., 1964).
1966   357 F. 2d 653-654 (5th Cir., Cert. denied, 384 U.S. 961.

Fisher, Sethard
1981   Race, class, anomie and academic achievement: A study at the high school level, *Urban education*, Vol. 16 (2), July pp. 149-174.

Finn, Chester
1981   *Wall Street Journal*, September 15.

Funston, Richard Y
1977   Constitutional counterrevolution? The Warren Court and the Burger Court: Judicial policy making in modern America. New York: Schenkman.

Gerard, Harold B. and Norman Miller
1976   School desegregation: A long-term study. New York: Plenum Press.

Green, Dr.
1971   The obligations of American social scientists. Annals of the American Academy of Political and Social Sciences, 395, pp. 13-27.

Hall, Mary H.
1968   A conversation with Kenneth B. Clark. *Psychology Today*, June, pp. 19-25.

Hart v. Community School Board
1975   New York School District No. 21, 512 F. 2d 37 (2d Cir.).

Hobson v. Hansen
1967   269 F. Supp. 401 (1967) at 406, 407.

Howe, Harold
1972   As cited in United Press International release, November 12.

Koestler, Arthur
1967   The Ghost in the machine. London: Hutchinson, pp. 272-293.

Kluger, Richard
1976   Simple justice. New York: Alfred A. Knopf.
Levin, Betsy and Philip Moise
1975   School desegregation litigation in the seventies and the use of
        social science evidence: An annotated guide. *Law and Contemporary Problems*. Duke University, School of Law, Vol. (1), Winter.
Mahan, Thomas W.
1966-68 Project Concern — 1966-68, A report on the effectiveness of
        suburban school placement for inner-city youth. Hartford, Connecticut, Board of Education.
Mahan, Thomas W. and Aline M. Mahan
1970   Changes in Cognitive style: An Analysis of the impact of white
        suburban schools on inner city children. *Integrated Education*, Vol. 8, p. 60.
1971   The impact of schools on learning: Inner-city children in
        suburban schools. *Journal of School Psychology*, Vol. 9 (1), pp. 1-11.
Maruyama, Geoffrey and Norman Miller
1979   Reexamination of normative influence processes in desegregated classrooms. *American Educational Research Journal*, Vol. 16 (3), pp. 273-283.
Mayer, Robert R. and James S. McCullough
1973   Social structural change and school performance. Department
        of City and Regional Planning, University of North Carolina, Chapel Hill, April 1973.
Mayer, Robert R. and Charles E. King, et al.
1974   The impact of school desegregation in a southern city. Boston:
        D.C. Heath.
Maynor, Waltz and W.G. Katzenmeyer
1974   Academic performance and school integration: A multi-ethnic
        analysis. *Journal of Negro Education*, Vol. 43, pp. 30-38.
Mosteller, Frederick and Daniel P. Moynihan
1972   On equality of educational opportunity. New York: Vintage
        Books.
Murphy, Gardner
1975   Outgrowing self deception. New York: Basic Books.
Nichols, Robert C.
1966   Schools and the disadvantaged. *Science*, Vol. CLIV, December
        9, 1966, p. 1314.
Phi Delta Kappan Editorial
1975   The prime goals of desegregation/integration are social justice
        and domestic tranquility. *Phi Delta Kappa*, April, 1975, p. 514.
Prichard, Paul N.
1969   Effects of desegregation on student success in the Chapel
        Hill school, *Integrated Education*, Vol. 7, pp. 33-38.
Prejudice and pride:
1979   The Brown decision after twenty five years, Washington, D.C.
        U.S. Department of Health, Education and Welfare.

Rist, Ray C. and Ronald J. Anson (Eds.)
1977 Education, social science and the judicial process. New York: Columbia Teachers College Press.
Rossell, Christina H.
1978 A response to the "white flight" controversy, *The Public Interest*, No. 53, Fall, pp. 109-115.
St. John, Nancy H.
1975 School desegregation outcomes for children. New York: John Wiley & Sons.
Schachtel, E.G.
1959 Metamorphosis. New York: Basic Books.
Schneider, E. Joseph
1981 School integration works for kids. *Educational Research and Development Report*, Vol. 4 (3), Fall, pp. 1-7.
Scott, Ralph
1966 First to ninth grade IQ changes of northern Negro students. *Psychology in the Schools*, Vol. III (2), April, pp. 159-160.
1975 The busing coverup: Can good intentions harm minority children? Rio, Wisc.: Martin Quam Press, pp. 97-106.
1979 School desegregation: A challenge to American social science? *Journal of Social and Political Studies*, Vol. 4 (1), Spring, pp. 67-69.
1981a Black achievement and desegregation: A research synthesis. Alexandria, Virginia: American Education Legal Defense Fund.
1981b Achievement effects of desegregation. Hearings before the Senate Subcommittee on Separation of Powers, September 30.
Stallings, Frank H.
1959 "A study of the immediate effects of integration of scholastic achievement in the Lousiville Public Schools," *Journal of Negro Education*, Vol. 28, pp. 439-444.
Stanley, Julian
1970 American Psychological Association Monitor, December 1970, p. 9+.
Stein, David
1974 Judging the judges: the cause, control and cure of judicial jaundice. Hicksville, N.Y.: Exposition Press.
Stephan, Walter G.
1978 School desegregation: An evaluation of predictions made in Brown v. Board of Education. *Psychological Bulletin*, Vol. 85 (2), pp. 217-238.
Taylor, William L.
1978 The Supreme Court and Recent School Desegregation Cases: The Role of Social Science in a period of judicial retrenchment, *Law and Contemporary Problems*. Duke University, School of Law, Vol. XLII (4), Autumn.
Weiss, Carol H.
1977 Using social research in public policy making. Lexington, Mass.: Lexington Books, p. 8.

Weinberg, Meyer
    1977   Minority students: A research appraisal. Washington, D.C.:
            U.S. Department of Health Education and Welfare. Parallel
            information appeared in "The relationship between school
            desegregation and academic achievement: A review of the
            research." *Law and Contemporary Problems*, Vol. 39, Winter
            1975 (1), pp. 240-270).
Weinstein, Eugene and Paul Geisel
    1963   Family decision making over desegregation. *Sociometry*, Vol.
            XXV (2), March, p. 28.
Wilkinson, J. Harvie III
    1979   From Brown to Bakke: The Supreme Court and Integration:
            1954-1978. New York: Oxford University Press.
Wilson, Kenneth L.
    1979   The effects of integration and class on black educational
            attainment. *Sociology of Education*, Vol. 52 (2), April, pp.
            84-98.
Wolf, Eleanor P.
    1977   Courtrooms and classrooms in Rist and Anson op. cit.
    1981   Trial and error: The Detroit school segregation case. Detroit:
            Wayne State University Press.

PLAYING THE SOCIAL SCIENCE CARD:
A NEW OPTION FOR NON-ACTIVIST ATTORNEYS?

Research into subsequent educational achievement by students in the now integrated school system has called into question the entire theoretical basis on which legally mandated school busing programs were based.

One of the most emotional and important issues in the U.S. over the past few decades has been the debate over court orders requiring the 'busing' of school children to achieve ad hoc ratios of black and white children in public schools around the nation. Under such court orders, children are transferred regardless of their wishes or the wishes of their parents, to schools in other neighborhoods in which the pupils are predominantly of a different race, in order to achieve a predetermined racial mix. The court justification for such orders generally rests heavily on opinions expressed by social scientists to the effect that black students will be able to learn better if placed in classes containing a substantial number of white children.

Recently I received a letter from a seasoned attorney, who seeks to avert forced busing in a major U.S. metropolitan area. He and I had previously sifted fact from fiction, with respect to desegregatory effects, and in his letter requesting additional information concerning the psychoeducational impact of busing on schoolchildren he writes: "As you know so well, the experts for the other side have a great tendency to be expansive and somewhat loose in their testimony."

Yes, I know that well. On various issues, the psychoeducational testimony has indeed been imbalanced. Within the courts, that imbalance has occured on such diverse topics as bilingual education, classroom quotas for gifted or retarded students, educational equity, forced busing, and fairness of tests. This paper briefly reviews historical evidence of academic bias and shows how this bias has contributed to erroneous judicial conclusions which have caused a backlash with some judges and, finally, summarizes how these developments create conditions whereby non-activist attorneys can effectively play the Social Science card, which in the past has invariably been used against them. The issues are complex and this paper focuses on a single question, one that has been, and is, central to a number of judicial rulings: How does busing affect minority learning?

Bias in Academia and in the Bureaucracy

Only through an examination of bias in academia is it possible to comprehend public and judicial understanding of desegregatory effects. It is widely assumed that social scientists are impartial and objective. In reality, this is simply untrue. Carol Weiss, drawing data from a Carnegie-funded study of attitudes within universities, surveyed 60,000 faculty members. Her conclusion: the overwhelming majority of social scientists seek to promote social change.(1) In an extension of Weiss' work, Eleanor Wolf studied expert testimony on desegregation and concluded that the academic community — by testimony on desegregation, by informal aid and consultation, or simply through refusal to aid defendants — has become the major reason why judges have ordered busing.(2)

Wolf suggests that objective court testimony, had it been presented, would have significantly reduced the scope and frequency of desegregation orders. But courts have rarely been given unvarnished desegregatory testimony, and Dr. James Coleman can explain why. In the 1960s, the U.S. Department of Health, Education and Welfare picked Coleman to appraise schooling effects.(3) His report turned up no evidence whatsoever that racial balancing of schools enhanced minority learning.(4) This was too big a surprise for even Coleman. He remained within academic respectability by inaccurately interpreting his own facts.(5)

Coleman has now done a turnabout, and said "The assumption that integration would improve achievement of lower class black children has now been shown to be fiction."(6) Coleman's reversal has evoked angry protests. Prominent academicians have urged social scientists to censure or to ignore him.(7) Nathanial R. Jones, NAACP General Counsel prior to being elevated to a Sixth Circuit Court of Appeals federal judgeship, was quoted by the *Detroit Free Press* as stating "Dr. James Coleman is a fraud...thoroughly repudiated by his colleagues." The media have distorted Coleman's position, characterizing him as "against desegregation" (with desegregation apparently defined as "forced busing") and "in favor of segregation." Coleman's voice is now all but stilled. He refuses to testify in desegregation cases.

The quality of testimony provided courts suffers when old

hands like Coleman are intimidated; it additionally suffers when editorial policies of "credible" professional publishing firms and journals exclude certain perspectives. Under such conditions, professors are discouraged from honestly reporting their research findings.

There are five major and interrelated reasons why editorial bias dissuades social scientists from objectifying desegregatory effects; 1) mainstream professional editors prefer articles which favor desegregation, and which cite evidence that busing appears to be working 2) publishing is a main artery to professional advancement; ambitious social scientists don't want to spend time writing material that won't be published 3) published books or articles produce greater public awareness, and public acceptance, of new positions; without credible publication, it is difficult for ideas (and their creators) to be included in the public forum. It follows that aspiring academicians are tempted to write on themes which conform with editorial bias 4) publications enable a professor to gain influence which can be exerted within the professions; "published" scholars are in a position to influence professional organizations; those organizations have invariably lined up political support for busing(8) and 5) influential publications can be persuasively used in courts of law.

Few attorneys or judges realize the extent to which busing is viewed as a "moral" issue within social science. And once an issue is moralized, inquiry stops. Coercion begins. Consider one example, which only illustrates how information about desegregatory effects can be restricted.

In 1982, a professor concluded an extensive investigation into the linkage between desegregation and black learning. The data revealed that busing fails to boost black learning. He submitted the article to one of the nation's leading influential journals. Eighteen months later, the journal's editor replied "....We concluded that your article is not appropriate. We would grant that academic achievement is important, but feel that at bottom the effort to desegregate the schools was based upon moral rather than academic considerations: those moral considerations seem not to have been mentioned. Those (including myself) who were ardent supporters of desegregation also thought in terms of other plausible benefits: altered life styles, increased incomes, better interracial understanding. None of these, of course, is strongly reflected in achievement scores." (9) This editor begs the question. A number of court cases have been predicted on the assumption that blacks would more effectively learn if they attended schools which were racially balanced. Hundreds of professional books and articles have been published, attesting to an alleged desegregation-black achievement linkage. It is impossible, of course, to ascertain the rejection rate of articles which demonstrated that busing did not enhance black learning.

If journals screen out certain views, and if professors are, in effect, coerced into conformity, then where do judges turn for objective appraisals of desegregatory effects? Presumably, the most objective source is the National Institute of Education (NIE), research arm of the Department of Education. But this agency has had trouble steering a straight course. Part of the problem lies with NIE reviewers who approach their task with bias: recently a proposal which sought to appraise long-term effects of desegregation was turned down. The NIE reviewer declared that such effects should not be studied. The Constitution, the reviewer declared, insists that schools be racially balanced. (10) However, the NIE has awarded dozens of grants to researchers who have concluded that busing improves minority learning. (11)

Fortunately, NIE activities are not limited to approval of academic reviewers. Some NIE projects are centered within the agency. But valid research efforts are thwarted even when this is the case. Thus in 1982 the agency appointed a blue ribbon panel to study the busing-black achievement relationship. (12) But the findings were squelched. The story reads like something out of the Soviet Union.

As NIE consultant, I concurred with agency representatives who insisted the panel be comprised of experts who represented various perspectives. With equity of bias controlled, the seven best-informed experts were selected. Moreover, the panelists were required to examine the same set of studies, and then to appraise the actual raw statistics upon which conclusions of each study had been based.

In July 1982, the panel gathered to select studies which met the necessary criteria. Initially 157 studies, considered the most prominent in the professional literature, were examined. Of these, only 18 (later expanded to 19) met even the crude inclusion requirements. The panel concluded, as Wortman noted, "...All of the individual studies have serious flaws ..."(13) This, obviously reflects the overall quality of desegregatory research. The panel noted that the winnowing process (from 157 to 19 studies) revealed that poorer quality studies invariably contained greater bias in favor of the view that desegregation enhances the black learning position. On the other hand, pro-busing bias was observed less frequently in the better designed studies; thus appears another index of prejudice within academia.

In December 1982, the NIE sponsored a panel discussion on the subject of desegregation (14). It was announced that the panelists' findings would be published in a monograph. As the session concluded, some federal officials expressed concern regarding the effect of the planned monograph, since the panels findings had not been supportive of desegregation. Some bureaucrats were angry and upset, and expressed apprehension that the NIE findings might "work their way into policy channels." One finding drew particularly intense fire: the panel was unable to identify a single longitudinal study which demonstrated that either voluntary or mandated desegregation significantly produced higher black learning profiles. More troubling still was evidence that mandated busing was linked with a *decline* in black learning.

In September 1983, NIE officials made four moves which assured obscurity for the panel findings. The agency 1) prematurely concluded the project 2) elected not to publish the monograph 3) broke its contract with the academic advisor who was credited with initiating the study and 4) terminated the NIE employee who had publicly stated that the panel "...had neither cleared up nor set-to-rest the central question" as to whether desegregation does facilitate black learning.

Courts: Victims of Inadequate Information?

The 1982-1983 NIE study is only the latest federally-funded examination into desegregatory effects which has been scotched for political reasons. Similar investigations, some as early as the mid-1960s, have demonstrated that desegregation fails to foster longitudinal black achievement gains.(15) But news of actual desegregatory effects is slow in reaching judicial circles. Thus Judge Julius L. Chambers has asserted that social scientists agree

that achievement gains will accrue from desegregation.(16)
In the landmark *Swann* ruling, Judge McMillan concluded
"...there is uncontradicted testimony..." that blacks will learn
better in racially balanced schools.(17) In *Milliken*, experts on
both sides agreed that racial balancing would upgrade minority
learning.(18) In 1983, litigation experts — who should know
better by now — testified that racial balancing would dramatic-
ally boost black learning.(19)

Beyond Bias: The Quest for Objectivity

What, then, is the bottom line? Are judicial rulings to be
divorced from research? Are remedies to be ordered, even when
they are neither wanted nor helpful? For attorneys who wish to
play the Social Science card, the outlook is decidedly bullish.
There are five basic reasons for this optimism.

1. Existing longitudinal data on desegregatory effects eases
the task of succinctly describing what busing does to students,
to school personnel, to parents, to schools, and to communities.
Equally important, claims of plaintiffs' experts can now be
more closely monitored, using those longitudinal facts. One
illustration: at a recent trial a nationally renowned expert was
asked to explain a series of tables he had presented to the court.
Astonishingly, he didn't understand his own tables. Moreover,
when those tables were explained to him (!!), they served the
defendants' case.

2. Predictions about busing effects have obviously gone awry
and are now being scrutinized as never before. The American
system permits a certain amount   of free exchange, ranging
from congressional hearings to individual litigation cases. Judges
and Congressmen (as well as media representatives) are more
likely to examine facts themselves, rather than naively trust the
experts.

3. Historically, fact-oriented social scientists have feared
testifying on busing. There was apprehension of being tar-
brushed "racist," should one testify that students fail to derive
benefits from busing. But the term "racist" has now been used
so often — applied to every President since Eisenhower —
that it has largely lost its inhibiting effects. This is particularly
true now that busing can no longer be validly depicted as a
"black vs white" issue. Solid busing opposition is registered by
black parents whose children have experienced busing reali-

ties.(20)

4. Despite persisting bias in key academic quarters, a growing body of literature documents actual busing consequences; to a certain extent this is related to awareness within some editorial circles that it is wise and timely — after several decades of imbalance — to retain some credibility by providing at least reference to the hidden side of desegregatory effects.

5. More than a few judges realize that they have been "used" with respect to social science. The NAACP is sensitive to this. Presently, the organization objects to granting black parents the right to have their children attend neighborhood schools, and also objects to introduction of evidence that busing impedes black learning.(21) This novel position finds the NAACP seemingly indifferent to remedies that are at best nonhelpful, and probably harmful, to black students. This NAACP stance has created a new mood with certain judges who have issued remedies which now lack credibility. And so Judge J. Skelly Wright has declared "a plague on the house of social science." Judge John Minor Wisdom and William E. Doyle insist that social science no longer effects busing decisions.(22)

Nowhere is the final product of inexpert expert testimony more apparent than in Boston. Here black parents oppose forced busing by a whopping 79%.(23) In the early 1970s Judge Arthur Garrity accepted, as fact, expert testimony attesting to alleged academic benefits black students would derive from busing. That testimony has returned to haunt him. Attorney Larry Johnson, representing the original black plaintiffs, faults Judge Garrity "because he did not make sufficient showing of improvements in desegregation and equal opportunity from desegregation."(24)

Judge Garrity, of course, had trusted establishment experts. In this respect, he joins with judges from across the country. However, not one of those judges wants to be in Garrity's shoes. That may be the best reason for nonactivist attorneys to play the Social Science card. More than ever before, and out of self interest, judges want to hear both sides of complex desegregatory questions. They don't want their information restricted, don't want to be ultimately sandbagged when their remedies are shown to be demonstrably counterproductive. Moreover, skillful use of the more carefully researched social science studies should not only enhance prospects for success by those seeking to curb social activism in areas such as the forced busing of school children out of their home localities; more significantly, such a move promises to insert a new definition of morality into the desegregation dispute, by demonstrating that "color blind" and neighborhood schools can deliver a higher quality of education for thousands of America's poorest and most vulnerable students.

FOOTNOTES

(1)   Weiss, Carol H. *Using social research in public policy making*. Lexington, Mass.: Lexington Books, 1977, p. 8.

(2)   Wolf, Eleanor P. *Trial and Error: The Detroit School Segregation Case*. Detroit: Wayne State University Press, 1981.

(3)   Coleman, James S. et al., *Equality of Educational Opportunity*. Washington, D.C.: U.S. Government Printing Office, 1966.

(4)   Dyer, Henry S. "School Factors and Equal Educational Opportunity," *Harvard Educational Review* 38: 38-56, 1968.

(5)   Coleman, James S. "The Meaning of Equal Educational Opportunity," In L.P. Miller and E.W. Gordon, (Eds), *Equality of Educational Opportunity*. New York: AMS Press, 1974, pp. 3-16. Also, *ER News, Educational Researcher* 2: 16-17, 1973.

(6)   Coleman, James S. "School Desegregation and City-Suburban Relations," Paper presented at Community College, Dearnborn, Michigan, April 21, 1978.

(7)   Orfield, Gary. "Research, Politics, and the Antibusing Debate," *Law and Contemporary Problems*, 42: 141-173, Autumn, 1978. Also, Clark, Kenneth. Social policy, power and social science research. *Harvard Educational Review, Vol. 43* (1), February, 1973, pp. 113-121. This article conveys rather explicit threats to academicians who disagree with Clark, the NAACP's central expert at *Brown*. Clark suggests that social scientists are willing to "compromise the fundamental humanity of dark skinned children and (who) by so doing provide public officials with rationalizations for regressive policies of malignant neglect...(thus becoming) agents of injustice. This role raises the serious question of whether social scientists and the type of research for which they are responsible should be permitted to have any direct role in decisions on important matters of equity, justice and equality of groups of human beings. Social scientists must set up an apparatus to monitor scrupulously their own work and involvement in matters affecting social policy. They must assume the responsibility for protecting a gullible public from the seductive pretentions of scientific infallibility which are now increasingly being offered. Social scientists must assume the difficult role of monitoring with vigilance the partnership of regressive politicians and social scientists."

(8)   Since the election of President Reagan, fact-oriented social scientists have sought to encourage federal policies receptive to open investigation of desegregatory effects within the National Institute of Education. Professional organizations have responded by charging that NIE is biased in placing "non qualified" personnel within the agency, a rather strange charge in view of evidence, since the NIE's research record is hardly impressive. For evidence of the interest professional organizations have taken with respect to the "politization" of NIE, see the June 4, 1982 letter to Terrell Bell, Secretary, Department of Education. This is signed by James G. Greeno, President, Federation of Behavioral, Psychological and Cognitive Sciences;

Michael S. Pallak, Executive Officer of the American Psychological Association; and William Cooley, President of the American Educational Research Association (AERA). Also, see Florio, David H. Education and the political arena: Riding the train, shaping the debate. *Educational Researcher*, official publication of the AERA, October, 1983, *Vol. 12* (8), pp. 15-16.

(9) Personal correspondence; identifying information is available upon request to qualified readers.

(10) Personal correspondence associated with a grant proposal submitted to NIE, 1982. Identifying information available to qualified readers upon request.

(11) NIE awards to investigators, who have reported a strong relationship between busing and black learning, are too numerous to mention. Some of these awards include: Crain, Robert L. and Mahard, Rita E. *Desegregation Plans that Raise Black Achievement: A Review of the Research*. National Institute of Education (N-1822-NIE), June 1982; Hawley, Willis D. and eight others. *Volume I: Strategies for Effective Desegregation: A Synthesis of Findings* (to be followed by at least eight other volumes). Vanderbilt University, April 1981 (Co-funded by NIE and the Office for Civil Rights).

(12) The Effect of School Desegregation on the Academic Achievement of Black Students, NIE, 1982-1983.

(13) Wortman, Paul M. Flaws in the studies of school busing. *Chicago Tribune*, June 2, 1983.

(14) Presentation of papers on desegregation and black learning, sponsored by NIE, Horace Mann Learning Center, FOB 6, Washington, D.C., December 17, 1982. For a description of this meeting, see "Slight academic gains made by blacks in desegregated schools: But scholars at NIE Forum disagree on significance of studies' findings," *Education Week*, February 16, 1983, p. 11.

(15) Scott, Ralph S. Jr. *Black Achievement and Desegregation: A Research Synthesis*. Washington, D.C.: American Education Legal Defence Fund, 1981, pp. 37-52; also, see *Education Daily*, September 24, 1975; additionally see *Prejudice and pride: The Brown decision after twenty-five years*, Washington, D.C.: National Academy of Education, 1979, p. 17.

(16) Chambers, Julius L. Implementing the Promise of *Brown*. In Ray C. Rist and Ronald J. Anson, *Education, Social Science and the Judicial Process*. New York: Teachers College Columbia University, 1977.

(17) Graglia, Lino A. "From Prohibiting Segregation to Requiring Integration: Developments in the Law of Race since *Brown*" in Walter G. Stephan and Joe R. Feagin (Eds), *School Desegregation: Past, Present and Future*; New York: Plenum Press, 1980.

(18) Wolf, Eleanor P. *Trial and Error: The Detroit School Segregation Case*. Detroit: Wayne State University Press, 1981.

(19) During 1983, experts testified in litigation in Mobile, Alabama and Kansas City, Missouri that busing would promote black learning (*Birdie Mae Davis, et al., vs. Board of School Commissioners of Mobile County, Alabama, et al.* and *Erica M. Black, et al., vs. State of Missouri*, respectively).

(20) Stephan, Walter G. and Feagin, Joe R. *School Desegregation: Past, Present and Future*. New York: Plenum Press, 1980; *New York Times*, June 21, 1982; Wilkinson, J. Harvie III. *From Brown to Bakke: The Supreme Court and School Intervention: 1954-1978*. New York: Oxford University Press, 1979; and Raffel, Jeffrey A. *One Year Later: Parent Views Toward Schools in New Castle County after the First Year of Desegregation*. Newark, Delaware: College of Urban Affairs and Public Policy, 1979.

(21) NAACP rejection of the option to provide black students with the opportunity to attend neighborhood schools is reported in : *Boston Globe*, March 5, 1982, and *Newsweek*, April 5, 1982; NAACP opposition to testimony involving possible harm to black youngsters who are bused appeared in *State of Missouri vs. Craton*

Liddell, et al. Also see NBC Nightly News, February 2, 1970; Gitelson, as cited in Sedlacek, W.E. and Brooks, G.C. *Racism in American Education.* Chicago: Nelson-Hall, 1976, p. 2; and Wisdom, John Minor. In Wilkinson, J. Harvie. *From Brown to Bakke: The Supreme Court and school integration: 1954-1978.* New York: Oxford University Press, 1979, p. 190.

(22) Wisdom, John Minor. In Wilkinson, J. Harvie. *From Brown to Bakke: The Supreme Court and school integration: 1954-1978.* New York: Oxford University Press, 1978, p. 190. And, Doyle, William E. Social science evidence in court cases. *Educational Forum,* Vol. 41, March 1977, pp. 263-270.

(23) *Boston Globe*, March 5, 1982. And, *Newsweek*, April 5, 1982.

(24) Scott, op. cit., p. 28. Also, See *Boston Globe*, March 5, 1982; *Newsweek*, April 5, 1982 and *Boston Herald*, October 16, 1983.

SCHOOL ACHIEVEMENT AND DESEGREGATION:
IS THERE A LINKAGE?

The author examines the latest evidence and finds that not only is there no justification for assuming that minority students benefit from integrated classrooms, but that forced busing apparently triggers events which retard the learning process for both minority and white students.

Does school desegregation enhance minority learning?* This question has been debated for more than a quarter-century, but social scientists remain divided and seem not to have gained an inch in the quest for reasonable consensus based on empirical fact. If, however, and as every president since Lyndon Johnson has claimed, desegregation is the most significant contemporary American educational issue, it would seem possible, in this age of computers, to resolve a relatively straightforward matter: achievement test scores should reveal whether the attainments of minority children improve as a result of desegregation. Sadly, such acquirable information is unavailable even to those who help shape national policy. Says William H. White (1978), staff director of the Office of National Civil Rights Issues of the U.S. Commission on Civil Rights: 'I'm unaware of any comprehensive study of school desegregation nationwide.'

The quest for verifiable information on desegregatory effects continues, although in a context marked by partisanship and controversy. In the fall of 1981, the U.S. Senate Subcommittee on the Separation of Powers invited four academicians to present evidence on the achievement effects of busing. The result was a two-two split, leaving the subcommittee of Senator James East with no apparent option but to use legislation as a tiebreaker. Commenting on the hearing, E. Joseph Schneider (1981), Executive Director of the Council for Educational Development, remarked 'It wasn't social science's best hour ... As the hearing ended, the social scientists shook hands all around while exchanging copies of their testimony. None seemed particularly bothered by the fact that the testimony, contradictory as it was, essentially nullified any social science influence on the proposed legislation.'

*As used here, desegregation refers to racial balancing of the public schools, which prohibits some children from attending their neighborhood school attendance center.

Disagreement among the Reviewers

In an effort to resolve conflicting research claims, the author examined findings reported in five major reviews of experiments concerning desegregation and minority achievement (Bradley and Bradley, 1977; Crain and Mahard, 1978; St. John, 1975;

TABLE 1

JUDGEMENT OF FIVE REVIEWERS

ACHIEVEMENT EFFECTS OF DESEGREGATION

In Eight Select Studies

	Judgement	
Study	Positive	Neutral
Anderson	St. John Crain Stephan	Weinberg (1968,1977) Bradleys
Evans (1969)		St. John Stephan Bradleys
(1971-73)	Weinberg (1977) Crain	
Mahan	St. John Weinberg (1977) Crain	Bradleys
Mayer	Stephan Crain Bradleys	St. John
Maynor (1970) With Katzenmeyer (1974)	St. John Stephan Crain	Bradleys
Prichard	Weinberg (1977) Crain	St. John Bradleys Stephan
Samuels	Weinberg (1968, 1977) Crain St. John	Stephan
Stallings	Weinberg (1968, 1977) St. John Stephan	Crain Bradleys

Stephan, 1978; Weinberg, 1977). At least four of the five reviews appraised the work of eight experiments whose work has been widely reported in desegregation literature (Anderson, 1966; Evans, 1969, 1972, 1973; Mahan, 1968, 1970, 1971; Mayer, 1973, 1974; Maynor, 1970, 1974; Pritchard, 1969; Samuels, 1958; and Stallings, 1959.) The findings of the eight researchers, who have sometimes worked with collaborators, is generally considered to provide the most convincing data that desegregation promotes black achievement. The first phase of this study, therefore, examined the conclusions reached in the five reviews with respect to the data obtained by the eight researchers and their colleagues. Results of this aspect of the present investigation are presented on Table 1.

Altogether and as shown on Table 1, the reviewers rendered 22 positive and 14 neutral judgements; no study was reported to have discerned desegregatory effects harmful to busing achievement, although the Bradleys (1977) and Stephan (1978) alluded to this possibility. Broken down by reviewer, the Bradleys considered 1 of 7 studies positive; for Crain-Mahard it was 7 of 8; Stephan 4 of 7; and Weinberg 5 of 6. The range of positive results therefore extended from 87.5% (Crain-Mahard) to 14.3% (Bradleys).

Clearly, the highly trained social scientists frequently disagreed as to just what effect desegregation has on black learning. In an attempt to comprehend these reported differences, the author proceeded to assess the primary data of the eight key researchers and their associates.

Dissecting Primary Data

Anderson's (1966) experiment, developed around his doctoral dissertation, contains a number of methodological flaws. Seventy-five pairs of students were matched (segregated, desegregated) for control purposes on the basis of age, sex, grade, intactness of family and third grade IQ scores; on page 2 of his introduction, however, he listed somewhat different matching criteria. Moreover, Anderson assumed the two populations (segregated, desegregated) would be equivalent with respect to second grade achievement tests. But different tests were used when members of the 1962-3 fourth, fifth and sixth grades were in second grade. Moveover, Tables 21 and 22 of Anderson's dissertation suggest that second grade achievement matching was not adequate. These tables list the T scores by grade on the *Metropolitan Achievement Tests* (April 1963) for students in segregated and desegregated schools, using a mean of 50 and a standard deviation of 10. For the first three student pairs cited (001, 002, 003), the comparative normative scores are 52.5 vs. 42.0; 56.5 vs. 40.3; and 59.5 vs. 42.0; each of these pairs is separated by more than a full standard deviation, all favoring the desegregated students. Such large differences run contrary to findings from comparable studies, and are open to doubt.

The open enrollment model used by Anderson created problems in obtaining an appropriate control population. Weinstein and Geisel (1963), for example, found that Nashville black families choosing desegregation for their children differed significantly from those who elected minority schools. Members of the latter group had less favorable attitudes toward 'pioneering' in race relations, were more socially alienated, and more apathetic and indifferent to social issues. These differences persisted when the effects of social class were partialed out. It is, therefore, unclear if Anderson's 'home background factor' — — determined solely on the basis of whether the family was intact — differentiated the children on the basis of those within-family dynamics which significantly shape learning behaviors. Parental choice for segregated or desegregated schools may in itself have been a differentiating factor.

Other methodological questions remain. The (75) matched pairs of students were apparently a highly select, and unrepresentative, group. Of the 1,500 students originally tested, only 10% (150, or 75 pairs) were included in the study. The mean IQs were 97.9 and 98.6 for desegregated and segregated subjects, respectively; these scores are substantially above the national mean for urban blacks. Anderson volunteered an additional problem: his statistical treatment violated one necessary statistical assumption — — that of randomness. Moveover, if the experiment did in fact reveal achievement gains, associated with integration, then other variables deserve attention in replication studies: for example, all the teachers in the desegregated schools were white. Current federal desegregation guidelines require not only busing, but also the racial balancing of teaching staffs. Desegregation adherents are just as concerned about (racial) teacher imbalances as student imbalances.

Summing up his study in an introductory overview, Anderson cautiously concluded that 'students in all five desegregated schools had higher mean achievement scores than did their counterpart groups. Differences in the amount of gains could easily be attributed to chance.' Pages 98 to 100 contain the statement:

'Desegregated students were classed into four levels of measured intelligence. All four desegregated groups had higher mean achievement scores than did their counterpart groups. Such differences in gains as did accrue could be attributed to chance ...'

In his investigation, Anderson also moved into the question of integration and race relations: he observed that blacks in desegregated schools evinced more marked anti-social tendencies than blacks in segregated schools. These differences, he noted, could easily have happened by chance.

Evans conducted three experiments, a doctoral dissertation (1969) and two subsequent studies for the Fort Worth Independent School District (1972, 1973). The dissertation data reveal either no difference with respect to learning trends of segregated and desegregated children, or negative findings in which the segregated children achieved higher scores.

Overall assessment of the Evans' later experiments reveal considerable student turnover. The 1971-2 study drew upon 552 bused and 634 nonbused pupils; one year later the respective figures were 349 and 428. Moveover the achievement effects were measured by grade equivalence with, for example, .5 signifying half a year of academic growth.

Consistently, the bused children started out with higher (prebusing) scores. For example, bused children in fourth and fifth grades scored .38 and .27 higher in reading (before desegregation) than their non-bused counterparts. Comparable pretest scores in math were .125 and .18, again favoring the bused students. The 1972-3 report indicated that in the spring of 1973, and in grades 3, 4 and 5, bused blacks achieved only .1 higher in reading than did the nonbused; in math the differences were .2 in the third grade, and .3 in both fourth and fifth grades. Considering initial differences, and the apparent evidence that the groups may have differed not only in achievement but also in home background factors, these differences seem either very small, or favor learning under neighborhood school circumstances.

Mahan (1968, 1970), chief researcher for Project Concern, initiated his data gathering in 1966; the program involved

TABLE 2

IQ CHANGES REPORTED OVER A TWO YEAR SPAN,
PROJECT CONCERN #

Grade completed in Spring 1968	Controls		Experimentals	
	Group I	Group II	Group III	Group IV
Grade I	3.0	--	8.2	9.3
Grade 2	2.0	--	5.0	2.6
Grade 3	3.3	0.5	5.4	6.7
Grade 4	-0.5	-4.2	6.4	6.2
Grade 5	6.7	-7.0	-2.2	2.6
Grade 6	3.3	-0.5	4.6	1.9

TABLE 3

IQ CHANGES, PROJECT CONCERN

Spring 1967-Fall 1967

	I	II	III	IV
K	2.0	--	4.4	8.1
1	-1.4	--	10.3	0.6
2	2.6	5.5	-3.3	2.9
3	2.8	-3.3	4.2	3.2
4	3.0	-1.3	-5.2	-0.5
5	<u>1.5</u>	<u>5.5</u>	<u>1.6</u>	<u>0.7</u>
	10.5	6.4	12.0	15.0

TABLE 4

IQ CHANGES, PROJECT CONCERN
Fall 1967 - Spring 1968

	I	II	III	IV
K	1.0	--	3.8	1.2
1	3.4	--	-5.3	2.0
2	0.7	-5.0	8.7	3.8
3	-3.3	-0.9	2.2	3.0
4	3.7	-5.7	3.0	3.1
5	<u>1.8</u>	<u>-6.0</u>	<u>3.0</u>	<u>1.2</u>
	7.3	-17.6	15.4	14.3

#Adapted from "A two year report: Project Concern." Hartford, Conn.:
Hartford Public Schools, August, 1968, Table 5, p. 23.

busing 266 black children from largely black schools in the north end of Hartford to 35 elementary schools in five suburban towns outside the city. The bused children, 266 in number, were selected randomly; no more than three were placed in any one class in any of the suburban schools. A control group of 305 nonbused children, selected from the same five sending schools, remained in the largely black schools. Experimental and control children entering grades 3 to 5 were further divided into two subgroups each. Special compensatory support was given to individuals in one of these subgroups; students in the other two subgroups were provided with only standard instruction. Thus, in the upper three grades, four groups were compared: Group I (nonbused, nonsupported); Group II (nonbused, supported); Group III (bused, nonsupported); and Group IV (bused, supported). Results from the project must be qualified because of design inadequacies. Group III consisted of only 4 children in grades 2 and 4 for example, and only 5 pupils in the third and fifth grade levels. Direct busing effects — where only desegregation served as an intervening variable — must be derived from comparative learning trends in Groups I and III. Data concerning progress of these groups are summarized in Tables 2, 3 and 4.

In examining IQ for each of the two years of busing as depicted on Tables 3 and 4 (Mahan. op. cit, 1968) it is useful to note the small number of children involved, and to recall the need to compare only Group I (nonbused, nonsupported) and III (bused, nonsupported) since only this comparison permits appraisal of busing-related learning changes.

Table 3 shows that during the first year of busing the cumulative differences between the two groups (I, III) are small (10.5 vs 12.0). If it were not for a large first grade gain (10.3) in Group III, the total gain (for all the busing years) would have been greater in Group I. Moreover, Table 3 shows that, during the first year of busing, desegregated children achieved higher gains in four grades of six (K, 1, 3, 5). But the differences at grades 3 and 5 are small indeed. During the second year (Table 4), desegregated students achieved higher scores in four grades (K, 2, 3, 5). Again, some of the differences fall short of practical significance. Also, if the second grade scores are striken from Table 4, the total IQ gains of Groups I and III are practically identical (6.6 vs 6.7).

As for achievement data, the *Metropolitan Readiness Test*

(MRT) was administered in kindergarten and grade 1; the *STEP Reading and Mathematics Test* was given in grades 3, 4, and 5, and no measures were obtained on grade 2. Achievement results reveal that only in one subtest (Alphabet), did kindergarten Group III (bused, non-supported) obtain significantly higher scores than Group I (not bused, non-supported). No significant differences obtained in the following other *MRT* measures: Word Meaning, Listening, Matching, Numbers, Copying and Total Score. Not a single significant difference was found at grade 1 and no achievement testing was done at grade 2. On grade 3, Group III significantly outperformed Group I in Reading and Mathematics, but at grade 4 Group I obtained significantly higher scores than Group III in Reading and Mathematics. Grade 5 scores show no statistically significant differences between Groups I and III. From these data, it appears that black children did about equally well in segregated or desegregated schools. In an effort to secure more information about this project, I wrote to the Hartford school superintendent who suggested that I write to Mr. William Paradis, coordinator of Project Concern. Two letters to Mr. Paradis failed to produce a response.

Mayer and his colleagues (1973, 1974) studied the effects of system-wide mandated desegregation in Goldsboro, North Carolina, which required the busing of blacks and whites; teachers and principals were also reassigned. In a number of respects Mayer qualified his findings. The study, he noted, was limited to two years and hence lacked the power of a longitudinal examination. Moreover, both blacks and whites improved in skill areas and he was uncertain whether or not this improvement could be attributed to desegregation, or to such factors as changes in the cultural environments transmitted by the mass media, new educational methods, or increased expenditures for schooling. He also found 'the data not at all encouraging' of the hypothesis that desegregation could reduce the racial achievement gap.

Mayer identified, for the major purpose of the study and as the most reliable index of desegregatory effects, results which are summarized on Table 5 and which employ a mean of 50 and a standard deviation of 10. Here it is noted that verbal scores of blacks increased from 38.6 to 41.8. However, the table also illustrates the value of longitudinal, as opposed to short-term, achievement experiments. For example, in 1970-71, blacks scored 1.6 points lower in reading than in 1968. Only when double-tested during the 1970-71 year (a practice rarely done, but conducted at Goldsboro because of the 'considerable disruption in normal school routines' associated with busing: double-testing may help students become 'test wise,' or may promote 'teaching to the test') did verbal scores of blacks rise. Also, and despite the double-testing, the table reveals an absence of black math gains associated with desegregation from 1968-69 (39.6) to 1971-2 (39.7). Mayer claimed that the disparity in math scores from second to third grade should be discounted, and that the predesegregation score in math should actually be 36.8 (1969-70 academic year). His reasoning: there was little math content in the second grade curriculum and math scores at that grade level tended to be unreliable. Whether or not one wishes to accept this explanation is perhaps a matter of taste, but has a direct bearing on St. John's (1975) conclusion that Goldsboro desegregation hiked math scores. Moreover, it is unclear whether the relatively small verbal gains of desegregated Goldsboro blacks might be associated not with desegregation but with such educational processes as teaching techniques employed in traditional classrooms.

Table five also shows that, taking the scores at face value, fifth grade Goldsboro blacks — the key research group — were performing at approximately a standard deviation below national norms. This suggests that desegregation has not significantly affected black achievements, particularly — racial comparisons are provided on Table 5 — if there has been an exodus of middle class whites who presumably score higher on standardized tests than their (white) lower class counterparts whose families are less likely to afford the luxury of moving, or having their children placed in private schools.

As St. John (1975) noted, some of (Mayer's) reported achievement improvements were related not to desegregation, but to teaching strategies. Mayer (1973) observed that, for every race and test group, those students who remained in traditional classrooms showed as great or, in some cases significantly greater improvement in achievement levels than did students experiencing the open classroom teaching style. On verbal scores, blacks in traditional classrooms showed an improvement of 4.41 achievement points compared to 1.89 in open classrooms. In math, blacks showed a gain of 3.54 in traditional classrooms compared with 0.33 in open classrooms. Thus if these figures can be translated into broad policy effects, black achievements might improve as a result of traditional teaching rather than from busing.

There is also value in appraising busing effects beyond achievement measures; Goldsboro schools have experienced disruption and increased disciplining of minorities since busing began. 'Middle class flight' has also been reported. Mayer began his study with an original student population of 667; three years later only 343, or slightly more than half the original experimental population, still attended Goldsboro schools; a disproportionate number of these were black.

Efforts have been made, unsuccessfully, to secure recent Goldsboro achievement scores from Superintendent William R. Johnson. A telephone call to Mr. Johnson's secretary disclosed that in the fall of 1979 the Goldsboro enrollment consisted of 3,880 (73 percent) black and 1,445 (27 percent) white. The 1970 guidelines, limiting black enrollment in any school to 62 percent, seem therefore to have become irrelevant. Social class resegregation seems to have taken place within the public schools. Because an estimated 75 percent of black and 25 percent of white children come from lower class families (Mayer, 1973) the Goldsboro schools have, since the initiation of busing, increasingly come to serve black and poor students.

Maynor (1970) and Maynor and Katzenmayer (1974) devised ambitious studies which sought to answer a number of questions. The central experimental question was whether achievement levels would decline in classes attended by students of different ethnic groups. Second priority was given to studying the effect of teacher's race on student learning. Only as a third priority were black achievement tends examined, and this question the experiment did not comprehensively address. The original Maynor experiment served as the basis of a doctoral degree and compared learning effects within the space of not more than eight months. The experiment was carried out in Hoke County, North Carolina, where, prior to desegregation, separate schools were maintained for black, Indian and white children. Desegregation, carried out in the fall of 1968, brought about the racial balancing of both students and faculty. The study therefore lacked an adequate control group. All elementary students attended the former Indian school; students in grades 6 to 8 were assigned to the former black school;

TABLE 5

Mean standard _SAT_ scores of second grade students in the
Goldsboro City Schools in 1968 who remained in the system
until 1972, by year, race, and subject area.

Year of Testing	Black Students		White Students	
	Verbal	Math Computation	Verbal	Math Computation
1968-69 2nd grade	38.6	39.6	45.0	50.1
1969-70 3rd grade	37.6	36.8	47.0	41.7
Total system desegregation				
1970-71 4th grade Fall	37.0	35.7	44.3	42.9
Spring	40.7	40.2	48.8	49.5
1971-72 5th grade	41.8	39.7	50.1	48.8

TABLE 6

Post-test Scores (mean 50, standard deviation 10)
Student-Teacher Pairings on
California Achievement Test Subtests

Students-Teachers Pairing	Reading	Language	Mathematics
White Students, White Teachers	58.2	57.7	56.2
White Students, Black Teachers	55.2	54.9	56.8
Black Students, White Teachers	44.9	45.5	45.0
Black Students, Black Teachers	43.9	43.6	45.9

TABLE 7

Means of Adjusted Post-Test Achievement Scores
for Black Students, instructed by
White, Indian and Black Teachers

	Teachers		
	White	Indian	Black
Reading	49.4	50.7	50.2
Language	49.8	52.6	49.9
Mathematics	49.9	52.4	50.1

grade 9 to 12 pupils attended the former white attendance center. Maynor's experiment also suffers from questionable use of test measures. *The California Achievement Test (CAT)* served as the pre- (Oct., 1968) and post-test (Spring, 1969) measure. Administration of the same measure over such a short interval invites contaminating test effects. Also, at post-testing, the *California Test of Mental Maturity (CTMM)* was given and used as an adjustment measure. Significantly, IQ measures are sometimes considered intervening desegregation variables. If the *CTMM* were to be employed as a control or adjustment measure, it should have been given at the time of pre- and not post- testing.

The central findings of the study, as summarized in a later paper prepared by Maynor and his colleague Katzenmeyer (1974), are on Table 6 — which groups students and teachers by race (white teachers with black and white students; black teachers with black and white students; since our survey is primarily concerned with black-white learning students, this table omits references to Indian students and teachers). Table 6 shows that in each subtest, at the time of post-testing, the black-white racial achievement gap exceeded the approximate national average of one standard deviation. Thus the Progressive Achievement Decrement (PAD)was not significantly different from the PAD in a typical segregated or desegregated school district.

Achievement scores were converted to standard scores, with a mean of 50 and standard deviation of 10 at each grade level for all races (black, Indian, white). Analysis of co-variance was then employed to compare post-test achievement (adjusted for intelligence and pre-test achievement scores), for each student pairing in each of the major achievement areas: Reading, Language and Mathematics. This procedure assumes an adjusted post-test score of 50, if within — race achievement trends remain the same before and after desegregation. If desegregation would increase learning, the adjusted scores should, therefore be greater than 50. Table 7 summarizes the means of adjusted scores for three groups of black students: those instructed by white, Indian or black teachers.

On Table 7 it is noted that blacks taught by white teachers did not measure up to predesegregation expectations in any of the three achievement areas. Black pupils taught by black teachers failed to derive significant educational benefits from desegregation; in all subject areas their (average) scores hover about the expectancy level of 50. Only when taught by Indian teachers did the black children perform in a manner suggesting the possibility that desegregation yielded practical achievement benefits. Replication studies are needed to determine whether this pattern would prevail in other school districts. In any event, these findings are not particularly encouraging: it is unlikely that conditions can, or should, be shaped so that large numbers of black students are taught by Indian teachers.

The Maynor-Katzenmayer data are discouraging along another dimension. The raw data from this study show that the achievement levels of black, white and Indian students declined during desegregation, if scores of black students with Indian teachers are omitted. Again employing the standard cutoff of 50 adjusted score, for example, the data show that in the overall experiment (race of students X race of teacher X academic area) only seven comparisons exceeded, and 17 fell below, the expectancy level of 50. 'Desegregated' blacks manifested twice as many academic declines as advances.

Summing up, results of the North Carolina experiments fail to support the contention that desegregation improved student learning. Regrettably, the raw data can no longer be studied: Maynor's dissertation is reported to be missing from the Duke University library.

Pritchard (1969) gathered data from students in Grades 5, 7 and 9, using as a control the data from the last year of segregation. Those scores were then compared with attainments of black students attending integrated schools for one or two years. Data from the study revealed no significant differences in reading achievement at any age level. Significant math differences did favor desegregated blacks at fifth and seventh grade. But Pritchard reported that the inauguration of a statewide curriculum revision in math may have influenced student math achievements. This obviously may have also affected teaching conditions. Thus the reported gains, limited to the mathematics area, may have had little if anything to do with desegregation.

Ivan Samuels' (1958) study derived from a doctoral dissertation which contains a number of research shortcomings. Comparisons were made concerning adademic performance of 45 children in desegregated, and 45 in segregated, schools of

New Albany, Indiana, at five grade levels (grades 1 through 4 and again in grade 6). Thus the average number of pupils per cell (treatment and grade level) was 9. Samuels sought to match the subjects by IQ (rather than achievement) but there was some mismatching. The means on the short form of the *California Short Form of Mental Maturity* were 96 and 87 for third graders, favoring the segregated.

On the first and second grade levels, results favored the segregated students on 13 of 14 measures. Three of the indices reached statistical significance. On the third grade level, only the total achievement scores (and no part scores) were statistically significant, favoring the desegregated. In the fourth grade the desegregated students achieved higher scores in six part scores and in Total Achievement.

Sixth grade desegregated blacks performed better, but the scores are in fact incredibly higher: the average of desegregated students stood at the 7.6 grade level on Language Usage whereas the segregated average for that portion of the test was 4.1, or 3½ years lower. In Arithmetic, the desegregated students obtained scores 1.8 grade levels higher than attainments of their segregated counterparts. These results are so contrary to nationwide trends that the entire design is subject to question, but further assessment is impossible because Dr. Samuels is deceased.

Summing up, if the scores on the Samuels' study are taken at face value then the study might be considered a draw: Results in grade 1 and 2 clearly favored segregated learning. A mixed pattern appeared with older children, but one which generally favors desegregation. Methodical problems — the lack of valid control on home background factors, the apparent mismatching of control and experimental groups, the low number of subjects involved, and some dramatic and questionable achievement increases of desegregated older students — combine to severely curtail the the value of the experiment.

Stallings' (1959) inquiry suffered from the type of subject control problem experienced by Anderson (1966). The study involved open enrollment, and equivalence of student samples was not determined. Home background factors were not controlled and, moreover, Stallings did not report his method of statistical analysis. Other variables serve to limit the value of the study as a vehicle for extending our understanding of the achievement-desegregation equation. The data were gathered over a period of less than a year. Perhaps the most telling flaw was Stallings' failure to compare achievement trends of bused and nonbused blacks; instead he employed a design which grouped students by race and then compared learning rates by race irrespective of whether individuals were bused or not. There was therefore no way to ascertain the extent in which learning profiles may have been exclusively associated with desegregation.

Busing: Does It Reveal Signs of Systems Failure?

The preceding analysis has revealed the extent to which prominent social scientists disagree concerning the interpretation of identical research studies. Assessment of the primary data produced by the eight targeted investigations has yielded no evidence, in any study, of verifiable long-term beneficial minority learning effects which can be definitively traced to busing. Findings of this synthesis indicate that social scientists may have erred in not placing higher priority on examination of primary data in appraisal of studies involving such sensitive issues as school desegregation.

The results of this survey suggest that overly optimist expectations have prevailed with respect to busing, especially since the reviews considered here have drawn on some presumably exemplary studies which are of two-decade vintage. There may be a logical explanation for the long-term acceptabillity of positive results which in fact did not exist. It might be argued that negative, although accurate, reports concerning the achievement-desegregation thesis might reduce public support for compensatory education efforts, and indeed such an interpretation largely muted the findings of Coleman (1978; Orfield, 1978) and Jencks (1972; Clark, 1973). The moralization of busing, however, ignores evidence that the nation's educational resources have been substantially and wastefully diverted into desegregation efforts for more than two decades, with no validated evidence of resulting benefits for students.

Presently, we witness evidence of a busing rollback. It is apparent that significant (anti-) busing legislation is being framed in Washington, and that judicial decisions are being tempered (Liddel vs. Board of Education, 1981). To some exent, reduced legislative and judicial support for busing may reflect growing disillusionment stemming from unrealized achievement expectations of desegregation. If so, then social scientists cannot lightly shrug off their responsibilities for the current state of affairs. Perhaps it is time to weigh the possibilities of a systems failure within social science, and the need for far-reaching reform. Such an examination might be painful and yet, ultimately, serve the best interests of all significant parties. For American youth, the stakes are far higher than the prestige of academia. For thousands of vulnerable students, education offers — or fails to offer — a last opportunity for development of competencies vital to adult job success.

REFERENCES

Anderson, Louis V.
    1966   The effect of desegregation on the achievement and personality patterns of Negro children. Unpublished doctoral dissertation, George Peabody College for Teachers University Microfilm, Nashville, Tennessee, 66-11, 237.

Bradley, Laurence A. and Gifford W. Bradley
    1977   'The academic achievement of black students in desegregated schools: A critical review.' *Review of Educational Research*, Vol. 47 (3), pp. 399-449.

Clark, Kenneth
    1973   'Social policy, power and social science research,' *Harvard Educational Review*, Vol. 43 (1), pp. 113-121.

        This article conveys rather explicit threats to academicians who disagree with Clark. One of Clark's statements is particularly noteworthy: after associating Jencks with a theory of genetic inferiority, Clark suggests that social scientists (such as Jencks) are willing to "compromise the fundamental humanity of dark skinned children and (who) by so doing provide public officials with rationalizations for regressive politics of malignant neglect...(thus becoming) agents of injustice. This role raises the serious question of whether social scientists and the type of research for which they are responsible should be permitted to have any direct role in decisions on important matters of equity, justice and equality of groups of human beings. Social scientists must set up an apparatus to monitor scrupulously their own work and involvement in matters affecting social policy. They must assume the responsibility for protecting a gullible public from the seductive pretentions of scientific infallibility which are now increasingly being offered. Social scientists must assume the difficult role of monitoring with vigilance the partnership of regressive politicians and social scientists."

Coleman, James S.
1978   School desegregation and city suburban relations. Paper presented at community college, Dearborn, Michigan.
Crain, Robert L. and Rita E. Mahard
1978   'Desegregation and black achievement. A review of the research.' *Law and Contemporary Problems*, Vol. 42 (3), pp. 17-56.
Evans, Charles Lee
1969   The immediate effects of classroom integration on the academic progress, self-concept and racial attitudes of Negro elementary children. Unpublished doctoral dissertation, North Texas State University, Denton, Texas.
1971   Short term desegregation effects: The academic achievement of bused students. Fort Worth Independent School District, Fort Worth, Texas (ERIC Document Reproduction Service No. ED 086 759).
1973   Integration evaluation: Desegregation Study II — academic effects on bused black and white students, 1972-73. Fort Worth Independent School District, Fort Worth, Texas. (ERIC Document Reproduction Service, No. ED 094 087).
Jencks, Christopher, et al
1972   Inequality: A reassessment of the effect of family and schooling in America. New York: Basic Books.
Liddell vs. Board of Eucation of St. Louis, Missouri, et al
1981
Mahan, Thomas W.
1968   Project Concern — 1966-68. A report on the effectiveness of suburban school placement for inner-city youth. Hartford, Connecticut, Board of Education.
Mahan, Thomas W. and Aline M. Mahan
1970   'Changes in cognitive style: An analysis of the impact of white suburban schools in inner city children.' *Integrated Education*, Vol. 8, p. 60.
1971   'The impact of schools on learning: Inner-city children in suburban schools.' *Journal of School Psychology*, Vol. 9 (1), pp. 1-11.
Mayer, Robert R. and Charles E. King et al
1974   The impact of school desegregation in a southern city. Boston: D.C. Heath.
Mayer, Robert R. and James S. McCullough
1973   Social structural change and school performance. Department of City and Regional Planning, University of North Carolina, Chapel Hill.
Maynor, Waltz
1970   Academic performance and school integration: A multi-ethnic analysis. Unpublished doctoral dissertation, Duke University.
Maynor, Waltz and W.G. Katzenmayer
1974   'Academic performance and school integration: A multi-ethnic analysis.' *Journal of Negro Education*, Vol. 43, pp. 30-38.

Orfield, Gary
    1978   'Research, politics and the antibusing debate.' *Law and Contemporary Problems*, Vol. 42, Part II. School of Law, Duke University.
Prichard, Paul N.
    1969   'Effects of desegregation on student success in the Chapel Hill school,' *Integrated Education*, Vol. 7, pp. 33-38.
St. John, Nancy H.
    1975   School desegregation outcomes for children. New York: John Wiley and Sons.
Samuels, Ivan G.
    1958   Desegregated education and differences in academic achievement. Unpublished doctoral dissertation, Indiana University.
Schneider, E.J.
    1981   'School integration works for kids.' *Educational Research and Development Report*, 4(3), pp. 2-7. Council for Educational Development and Research.
Stephan, Walter G.
    1978   'School desegregation: An evaluation of predictions made in *Brown v. Board of Education*,' *Psychological Bulletin*, Vol. 85 (2), pp. 217-238.
Stallings, Frank H.
    1959   'A study of the immediate effects of integration on scholastic achievement in the Louisville Public School,' *Journal of Negro Education*, Vol. 28, pp. 439-444.
Weinberg, Meyer
    1975   Minority students: A research appraisal. Washington, D.C.: U.S. Department of Health, Education and Welfare.
Weinstein, Eugene and Paul Geisel
    1963   'Family decision-making over desegregation.' *Sociometry*, XXV (2), p. 28.
White, William H.
    1978   *Christian Science Monitor*; personal communication, October 18, 1979.

SEX AND RACE ACHIEVEMENT PROFILES IN A
DESEGREGATED HIGH SCHOOL IN THE DEEP SOUTH

The author examines SAT scores by sex and race and concludes that the
gap between blacks and white is under-represented by SAT results because of
the very high percentage of white students who obtain the maximum score.

In *Brown vs Board of Education* (1953-1954), the U.S.
Supreme Court leaned on social science for its central thesis
in ruling that segregation damaged the personal and mental
development of black students.(1) Since that time, social
policymakers have confidently assumed that black learning
levels would be raised if the racial composition of a student
body were racially balanced.

It now appears that there never was any evidence that racial
balancing of the schools would promote learning of black
students. If the practice yields neither educational nor social
gains, and if it is often carried out against the express desires of
minority and majority parents, it should be possible to identify
why expensive and disruptive racial balancing continues, and
presently no logical explanation has been forthcoming; instead,
highly placed educators and government officials continue to
insist — without empirical support — that black learning is
increased by reassigning students from neighborhood schools to
distant attendance centers, solely on the basis of race. This
article summarizes evidence, consistent with data he has previously reported, that long-term mandated desegregation in the
United States has not enhanced black learning.

For unknown reasons, it is only recently that American
social scientists have begun to seriously question the desegregation-black achievement thesis. A blue ribbon committee of the
National Institute of Education, research arm for the Department of Education, was unable to identify a single study which
demonstrated that busing authentically enhances black learning.(2) Moreover, there is some evidence that desegregation may
be educationally counterproductive. St. John has suggested
that the racial achievement gap may contribute to blacks'
higher anxiety levels in integrated academic settings where more

(1) *Brown vs. Board of Education*, 347 U.S. 483 (1953-54).
(2) Uribe, O. The effects of school desegregation on the academic achievement of
black students. Washington, D.C.: National Institute of Education, September 1983.

rigorous academic requirements may prevail,(3) a perspective to which other researchers have lent credibility.(4, 5, 6) St. John's thesis has been extended by Coleman, major author of *Equality of Educational Opportunity*,(7) who now concludes that busing is probably harmful to vulnerable black students.(8)

The assumption that racial balancing by itself enables black students to raise academic competencies was tested, however in-advertently, in *Debra P. vs. Turlington*, which has the potential of influencing educational promotion policies in 36 states.(9) In this Florida litigation, U.S. District Court Judge George Carr originally ordered a four year delay in implementing literacy tests. Carr thus concurred with an NAACP complaint that literacy tests would deny a disproportionate number of minor-ity students their high school certificates and he forbade Florida school officials from making literacy tests a graduation require-ment until all vestiges of school segregation were gone. Further, Carr ruled that in four years, and after the 1979 black freshmen had the educational benefits of a totally desegregated high school, the test would no longer be considered discrimina-tory.(10)

Four years after his original order, Carr lifted the ban on withholding diplomas for the 1300 students who had failed the state's functional literacy test. Of those who failed, 62% were black although blacks constitute only 21-22% of the state's high school population.(11) These statistics raise questions concerning the original NAACP contention that four years of desegregated schooling would narrow the ethnic achievement gap. However, four years is a relatively short period of time; the

(3) St. John, N.H. *School desegregation outcomes for children.* New York: John Wiley and Sons, 1975.

(4) Gerard, H.B. and Miller, N. *School desegregation: A long-term study.* New York: Plenum Press, 1975.

(5) Patchen, M.; Hofmann, G.; and Brown, W. Academic performance of black high school students under different conditions of contact with white peers. *Sociology of Education*, January 1980, *53* (1), 33-51.

(6) Scott, R.S. Mandated desegregation and black students' anomie: Summary of the empirical evidence. Paper prepared for the Office of the Attorney General, State of Missouri, February 15, 1982.

(7) Coleman, J.S., et al. *Equality of educational opportunity.* Washington, D.C.: U.S. Government Printing Office, 1966.

(8) Coleman, J.S. School desegregation and city suburban relations. Paper pre-sented at Community College, Dearborn, MI, April 21, 1978.

(9) *Debra P. vs. Turlington, 474 F. Supp. 244* (M.D. Fla. 1979).

(10) Ibid., Aff'd in part and vacated and remanded, *644 F2d 397* (5th Cir. 1981).

(11) *Integrated Education*, Issues 121-126, January-December 1983, p. 263.

Table 1

Means and Standard Deviations for Total Sample by Sex, by Race and by Sex x Race

	All S	Sex		Race		Sex x Race			
		M	F	Bl	Wh	MB	MW	FB	FW
R (Voc)	10.6 2.4	10.7 2.3	10.5 2.5	9.0 2.3	11.6 1.9	9.2 2.4	11.7 1.6	8.8 2.2	11.6 2.1
R (Comp)	10.8 2.6	10.9 2.6	10.8 2.5	9.2 2.8	11.9 1.7	9.5 3.0	11.8 1.9	8.8 2.5	12.0 1.6
R (Total)	10.8 2.3	10.9 2.2	10.8 2.4	9.2 2.3	11.8 1.6	9.6 2.3	11.8 1.7	8.9 2.3	11.9 1.6
Spelling	10.6 2.6	10.1 2.7	11.0 2.4	9.9 3.0	11.0 2.2	9.1 3.0	10.7 2.3	10.6 2.8	11.2 2.1
L (Mech)	10.6 3.2	11.0 3.5	10.2 2.8	8.8 3.0	11.3 2.8	8.4 2.8	11.4 2.2	9.1 3.1	12.2 3.3
L (Exp)	11.1 2.5	11.2 2.3	11.1 2.7	9.7 3.0	12.0 1.7	10.0 2.6	12.0 1.7	9.3 3.3	12.1 1.7
L (Total)	11.1 2.5	11.0 2.4	11.1 2.6	9.5 2.7	12.0 1.6	9.5 2.5	11.9 1.7	9.4 3.0	12.1 1.6
M (Comp)	11.4 1.7	11.4 1.6	11.3 1.8	10.7 1.9	11.8 1.4	10.8 1.8	11.9 1.3	10.7 2.0	11.7 1.5
M (Concepts & Applications)	11.0 2.1	11.2 1.9	10.3 2.2	9.9 2.1	11.7 1.8	10.0 1.8	12.0 1.6	9.7 2.2	11.5 2.0
M (Total)	11.2 1.7	11.3 1.6	11.1 1.8	10.3 1.8	11.7 1.4	10.3 1.6	11.9 1.2	10.2 2.0	11.5 1.5
Total Battery	11.2 2.0	11.2 1.9	11.2 2.1	9.9 2.0	12.0 1.5	9.9 1.8	12.1 1.4	9.8 2.2	12.0 1.6

questions of desegregatory achievement benefits is more legiti-
mately framed by examining the ethnic achievement gap in a
sampling of black and white students who have attended
desegregated schools throughout their primary, and well into
their secondary, school years. This paper, therefore, appraises
the racial achievement gap observed in a sampling of high school
students who, except for transferees from racially imbalanced
schools, have only attended desegregated schools.

Method

Achievement scores resulting from the spring 1983 group
administration of the *California Achievement Test (CAT)* were
obtained on all tenth grade students attending a metropolitan
high school of the deep South; all elementary and secondary
schools of the district had been desegregated since the early
1960s. The school district serves a large geographic area which
has grown in population and in affluence during the past
several decades. Names of all tenth grade students were alpha-
betized and the first seven students from each alphabetic cluster
of ten were designated for inclusion in the study. Following this
randomization of 70% of the student body, school officials
identified the sex and race of individual students. This process
resulted in a sampling of 210 whites (97 male, 113 female) and
133 blacks (64 male, 69 female). The sample approximated the
ethnic distribution of the school, which was 60% white and 40%
black. On each of the *CAT* subtests, as well as for the Total
Battery, means and standard deviations were obtained for all
subjects by sex and by race, and also race x sex. Analysis of
variance was employed to appraise the extent of variance
attributable to sex, to race, and to the interaction of sex and
race. Finally, the incidence of students, by sex and race, who
attained maximum scores on the *CAT* was obtained.

Results and Discussion

Table 1 summarizes the means and standard deviations for all
subjects, by sex, by race, and by interaction of sex x race. This
table shows that average scores for all students were at, or in
excess of, national norms: for example, in Reading (Vocabulary) the average for all subjects in the sample was 10.6, or the

Table 2

Analysis of Variance
California Achievement Test Scores, by sex

	Sum of Squares		DF		Mean Square		F	Sig.
	Between Groups	Within Groups	Between Groups	Within Groups	Between Groups	Within Groups		
R (Voc)	3.9	1986.9	1	341	3.9	5.8	0.7	.42
R (Comp)	.6	2239.5	1	341	.6	6.6	0.1	.76
R (Total)	2.5	1807.1	1	341	2.5	5.3	0.5	.50
Spelling	69.6	2221.2	1	339	69.6	6.6	10.6	.00
L (Mech)	55.1	3510.5	1	339	55.1	10.4	5.3	.02
L (Exp)	.3	2126.1	1	330	.3	6.4	.1	.82
L (Total)	1.7	1989.5	1	324	1.7	6.1	.3	.60
M (Comp)	.8	943.4	1	330	.8	2.9	.3	.60
M (Concepts & Applications)	12.1	1464.6	1	330	12.1	4.4	2.7	.10
M (Total)	3.5	942.0	1	330	3.5	2.9	1.2	.27
Total Battery	0.1	1272.5	1	322	0.1	4.0	0.2	.90

sixth month of tenth grade. Table 1 also indicates that males and females generally attained somewhat similar scores in the various achievement areas: there are two notable exceptions to this inasmuch as females outperformed males in spelling by nearly a full grade equivalency while a contrary trend is noted in Language (Mechanics) wherein males did better. Large ethnic achievement differentials appear on Table 1, but the ethnic gap appears to be appreciably smaller in Spelling (1.1 grade levels) and most substantive in Reading (Total) where a differential of 3.6 grade levels obtains. This table also reveals that in most achievement areas black males outperformed black females, but the trend was reversed in several achievement areas and most prominently in Spelling where black females outperformed black males by 1.5 grade levels. Despite a tendency for white males and white females to score quite similarly in most subjects areas, white females outperformed white males in Language (Mechanics) by .8 of a grade level.

Table 2 shows that sex differences were statistically significant on only two of the CAT subtest measures, Spelling and Language (Mechanics). Reference to Table 1 shows that the sex differences in Spelling are largely attributable to the fact that white males obtained significantly higher scores than black males; however, black females scored approximately the same as white males on this subtest; therefore, the sex differences are largely ascribable to the low scores attained on this subtest by black males, a finding which may hold important curricular implications.(12) Again referring to Table 1, there is reason to believe that the significantly higher female scores in Language (Mechanics) are largely attributable to the higher scores of white females over their race counterparts (3.1 grade levels). Attainments of white males fell short of white females, but a large male gender gap (3.0) is also noted.

Large and statistically significant differences are observed on every CAT measure on Table 3, which summarizes analysis of variance by race. However, ethnic differences are substantially narrower in Spelling and Mathematics (Comp.), while they are largest in the Reading measures.

(12) Murray, C. Losing ground: American social policy 1950-1980. New York: Basic Books, 1984. Also, see Danziger, S. and Gottschalk, P. Helping the poor help themselves. The Wall Street Journal, May 21, 1985, p. 34. It is predicted that poverty rates for blacks will continue to exceed 30% unless significant improvements are made in various social delivery systems.

Table 3

Analysis of Variance
California Achievement Test Scores, by race

| | Sum of Squares | | DF | | Mean Square | | F | Sig. |
	Between Groups	Within Groups	Between Groups	Within Groups	Between Groups	Within Groups		
R (Voc)	568.3	1422.4	1	341	568.3	4.2	136.2	.00
R (Comp)	603.4	1636.7	1	341	603.4	4.8	125.7	.00
R (Total)	554.1	1255.5	1	341	554.1	3.7	150.5	.00
Spelling	96.2	2194.6	1	339	96.2	6.5	14.9	.00
L (Mech)	737.6	2827.9	1	339	737.6	8.3	88.4	.00
L (Exp)	438.3	1688.2	1	330	438.3	5.1	85.7	.00
L (Total)	512.8	1478.4	1	324	512.8	4.6	112.4	.00
M (Comp)	80.3	863.9	1	330	80.3	2.6	30.7	.00
M (Concepts & Applications)	276.6	1200.1	1	330	276.6	3.6	76.1	.00
M (Total)	161.3	784.2	1	330	161.3	2.4	67.9	.00
Total Battery	351.3	921.3	1	322	351.3	2.9	122.7	.00

Table 4 summarizes analysis of variance results, by sex and by race. These findings show that ethnic achievement differences are far more extensive than those associated with sex. For example, in Reading (Vocabulary) the significance for Main Effects of Sex is .24 which is statistically insignificant; for Race the Main Effects are significant at the .01 level. Moreover, Two-Way Interactions of Sex x Race are statistically insignificant (.45). Similar trends are observed on each CAT measure, and demonstrate powerful ethnic effects.

Finally, Table 5 summarizes the number and percent of students who attained maximum scores on the CAT, by sex and race. In Reading (Vocabulary) for example, 12.5% of male blacks, 53.6% of male whites, 8.7% of female blacks and 59.3% of female whites attained the maximum score of 12.9 grade equivalency. It is apparent from Table 1 that in each tested area a high proportion of students, an inordinate number of them white, secured the maximum scores.

Summary

This study has examined tenth grade scores in a school district of the deep South which has been desegregated for more than 15 years. Results reveal that, in the areas measured by the CAT, sex and race achievement gaps assume quite different profiles. With only a few exceptions, sex differences are statistically insignificant; males attained slightly higher scores in most subtests. However, the only statistically significant differences were in Spelling and Language (Mechanics), with females attaining higher scores on the former, and males on the latter.

Large and statistically significant ethnic differentials appear in all CAT categories. However, the magnitude of the racial gap varied considerably, being narrowest in Spelling and Mathematics (Computation) and widest in Reading. If replication studies affirm these findings, differentials in ethnic achievement gaps may hold useful curricular implications. It also appears noteworthy that black males outperformed black females in Reading and Language (Expression), whereas black females did better in Spelling and Language (Mechanics).

Data of this study provide no evidence whatsoever that long-term desegregation has narrowed the ethnic achievement gap. Indeed, these results suggest that use of the CAT has produced

Table 4

F and Significance of F, Analysis of Variance
California Achievement Test Scores, by sex & race

	Main Effects	Sex	Race	Interaction, Sex x Race
R (Voc)	68.8 (.00)	1.4 (.24)	139.7 (.00)	.6 (.45)
R (Comp)	63.3 (.00)	.3 (.57)	126.4 (.00)	3.0 (.08)
R (Total)	76.2 (.00)	1.1 (.29)	151.7 (.00)	2.7 (.10)
Spelling	13.0 (.00)	10.7 (.00)	14.9 (.00)	3.3 (.07)
L (Mech)	45.6 (.00)	5.2 (.02)	84.5 (.00)	.02 (.90)
L (Exp)	42.2 (.00)	.6 (.43)	84.2 (.00)	2.1 (.15)
L (Total)	56.0 (.00)	.1 (.81)	111.6 (.00)	.5 (.47)
M (Comp)	15.6 (.00)	.6 (.43)	30.9 (.00)	.1 (.78)
M (Concepts & Applications)	40.9 (.00)	4.9 (.03)	78.4 (.00)	.2 (.64)
M (Total)	35.3 (.00)	2.5 (.12)	69.1 (.00)	.5 (.49)
Total Battery	61.2 (.00)	.3 (.61)	122.3 (.00)	.0 (.91)

an unusual profile of achievement test results, characterized by elevation of both black and white scores. The long upper tail of the skewed curve is severed below the white mean; if the CAT possessed normal psychometric features which would necessarily include both long lower and upper tails, then the racial achievement gap would have been still wider than that reported here.

Many school districts employ the CAT, and have reported enhancements of black scores subsequent to desegregation. Findings of this investigation indicate that such encouraging reports are based on test scores which obscure the actual magnitude of the racial gap and which, therefore, are likely to produce the reassuring but false and ultimately disillusioning belief that students' school attainments are higher than they are in fact.

These CAT results reveal an enormous potential for misleading policymakers. More than half of all white students obtained a maximum score on each CAT measure, and in Mathematics (Total) fully 76% of white males attained maximum scores. There are educational reasons why achievement tests may not have an inordinately long upper tail since they are primarily designed to assess achievement at a given grade.(13) Skills and information targeted for the higher grades are often excluded, but only up to a point, since inter-student variability is a key ingredient of a valid achievement measure and of subsequent instructional strategies. However, when a majority of high school tenth graders score at levels reportedly commensurate with norms for graduating seniors, basic questions must be asked. Of course it is possible for high scores to prevail when students are exceptional; but the proportion of students in this study who secured superior scores on the CAT is particularly perplexing when consideration is given to the phenomenon of middle class flight from the public schools which, often observed in school districts subjected to mandated busing, has left the public schools serving a higher proportion of poor and minority students, and fewer of the highest achieving youth.(14, 15)

Despite the apparent tendency of the CAT's low ceiling to

(13) Jensen, A.R. *Bias in mental testing*. New York: Free Press, 1980, p. 96.
(14) McMillan, R. That busing success story. *The Wall Street Journal*, January 21, 1985.

Table 5

Number and Percent of Students Attaining
Maximum Scores on California Achievement Test, by Sex and Race

	Male Black	Male White	Female Black	Female White
R (Voc)	N 64 Max. 8 12.5%	N 97 Max. 52 53.6%	N 69 Max. 6 8.7%	N 113 Max. 67 59.3%
R (Comp)	N 64 Max. 17 26.6%	N 97 Max. 64 66.0%	N 69 Max. 12 17.4%	N 113 Max. 74 65.5%
R (Total)	N 64 Max. 10 15.6%	N 97 Max. 58 59.8%	N 69 Max. 9 13.0%	N 113 Max. 67 59.3%
Spelling	N 63 Max. 17 27.0%	N 96 Max. 48 50.0%	N 69 Max. 41 59.4%	N 113 Max. 71 62.8%
L (Mech)	N 63 Max. 8 12.7%	N 96 Max. 54 56.3%	N 69 Max. 19 27.5%	N 113 Max. 81 71.7%
L (Exp)	N 63 Max. 14 22.2%	N 92 Max. 61 66.3%	N 64 Max. 17 26.6%	N 113 Max. 81 71.7%
L (Total)	N 61 Max. 12 19.7%	N 91 Max. 60 65.9%	N 64 Max. 18 28.1%	N 110 Max. 82 74.5%
M (Comp)	N 63 Max. 26 41.3%	N 92 Max. 69 75.0%	N 65 Max. 30 46.2%	N 113 Max. 78 69.0%
M (Concepts & Application)	N 63 Max. 13 20.6%	N 92 Max. 64 69.6	N 65 Max. 13 20.0%	N 113 Max. 62 54.9%
M (Total)	N 63 Max. 17 27.0%	N 92 Max. 70 76.1%	N 65 Max. 21 32.3%	N 113 Max. 72 63.7%
Total Battery	N 60 Max. 8 13.3%	N 90 Max. 58 64.4%	N 64 Max. 13 20.3%	N 110 Max. 72 65.5%

compress the ethnic gap and to elevate scores, results from this investigation indicate that the ethnic gap is as high or higher than that reported during the predesegregation era. In 1966 Coleman reported an average difference of 2.4 years at grade nine, and 3.3 years at grade 12.(16) The present study reveals an ethnic gap of 3.6 years in Total Reading and 2.1 years in Total Battery, even though approximately 60% of all white students obtained a maximum (12th grade) score on both measures. When standard deviation units are applied to the data obtained by Coleman and to scores of the tenth grade students in this study, the ethnic gap is larger for the latter. This researcher, therefore, concludes that the failure of *CAT* achievement scores to properly measure the gap between White and Black students could easily delude policy analysts into attributing illusionary academic benefits to desegregation; if so, and in view of enormous problems encountered by job-seeking minority youth,(17) the ultimate results could easily be counterproductive.

(15) Scott, R.S. School desegregation: A challenge to American social science. *Journal of Social and Political Studies,* Spring 1979, *4* (1), 67-79. (Selected for referencing in *Sociological Abstracts,* International Sociological Association, Fall 1979.)

(16) Coleman, op. cit., 1966, pp. 20-21.

(17) Sieber, S.D. *Fatal remedies: The ironies of social intervention.* New York: Plenum Press, 1981; also, see Special report: The full extent of the disaster. *Behavior Today,* April 14, 1980, 1-2.

MANDATED SCHOOL BUSING AND STUDENT LEARNING: ACHIEVEMENT PROFILES OF THIRD, FIFTH AND TENTH GRADE BLACK AND WHITE STUDENTS

U.S. legislation mandating sweeping and costly measures designed to ensure racial integration in school classrooms, was originally based on unproven academic hypotheses that the wide gap between white and black pupils in scholastic achievement tests would be reduced if blacks were to study alongside whites in classrooms. After a generation of racially integrated education, U.S. schools still reveal dramatic gaps in test scores between whites and blacks, indicating that the reason for the marked disparity in educational achievement that persists between the members of disparate ethnic groups has not been modified by the legally enforced integration of classrooms.

For more than three decades, educators and the courts have generally assumed that black students would more effectively learn under desegregated circumstances, and that the racial gap would decline in response to racial balancing of the public schools. Such assumptions were endorsed by social scientists throughout proceedings of *Brown*, the landmark Supreme Court desegregation case of the 1950s and in subsequent litigation.(1) In *Hobson vs Hanson* (1967), and in response to persuasive expert opinion, Judge J. Skelly Wright stated "Racially and socially homogeneous schools damage the minds and spirits of all children. The scholastic achievement of the disadvantaged child, Negro and white, is strongly related to the racial and socioeconomic composition of the student body. A racially and socially integrated school environment increase the scholastic achievement of the disadvantaged child of whatever race..."(2) In *Milliken*, experts on both sides agreed that racial balancing would promote minority learning.(3) Judge James McMillan, in his 1969 ruling concerning the schools of Charlotte-Mecklenburg County, North Carolina, expressed surprise that a black-white achievement gap existed. Further, he referred to the un-contradicted testimony of the experts and administrators who all agreed that (racial balance) produced a dramatic improve-

(1)   *Brown vs. Board of Education, 347 U.S. 483 (1953-54).*
(2)   *Hobson vs. Hansen, 169 F. Supp. 401 (1967) at 406-07.*
(3)   Wolf, Eleanor P. Courtrooms and Classrooms. In Rist, Ray C. and Anson, Ronald J. (Eds.) *Education, Social Science and the Judicial Process.* New York: Teacher's College Press, 1977, p. 101.

Table 1

Third Grade Students' Grade Equivalency Scores, Means and Standard Deviations:
by Sex, Race, and Sex X Race

	All Ss (N107)	Sex		Race		White - Black Male		White - Black Female	
		M (N48)	F (N59)	W (N67)	B (N40)	WM (N28)	BM (N20)	WF (N39)	BF (N20)
R-VOC	4.0 1.3	3.8 1.4	4.2 1.2	4.5 1.4	3.3 1.2	4.3 1.2	3.1 1.2	4.6 1.1	3.4 0.9
R-CM	4.2 1.4	3.9 1.4	4.4 1.3	4.7 1.3	3.3 0.9	4.3 1.4	3.2 1.1	4.9 1.2	3.4 0.8
R-TL	4.2 1.6	4.0 1.7	4.5 1.4	4.9 1.5	3.3 1.1	4.6 1.7	3.1 1.2	5.1 1.3	3.5 0.9
Spelling	5.6 2.7	4.9 2.5	6.2 2.7	6.1 2.7	4.8 2.4	5.2 2.4	4.6 2.6	6.7 2.7	5.0 2.1
L-MC	5.4 2.0	4.7 2.0	6.0 1.8	5.8 1.9	4.9 2.0	5.0 1.9	4.3 2.0	6.3 1.7	5.4 1.8
L-EX	4.3 1.8	3.6 1.5	4.8 1.9	4.8 1.9	3.5 1.3	4.1 1.6	2.9 1.1	5.2 1.9	4.0 1.3
L-Total	5.1 2.0	4.2 1.7	5.7 2.0	5.6 2.0	4.0 2.7	4.7 1.8	3.6 1.5	6.2 2.0	4.8 1.7
M-CM	4.3 0.7	4.1 0.8	4.4 0.7	4.4 0.7	4.0 0.7	4.2 0.8	3.9 0.7	4.5 0.7	4.1 0.6
M-CN	4.0 1.1	3.7 1.2	4.2 1.0	4.3 1.1	3.4 1.0	4.0 1.2	3.3 1.0	4.5 0.9	3.6 0.8
M-Total	4.1 0.9	3.9 0.9	4.3 0.8	4.4 0.9	3.8 0.8	4.1 1.0	3.6 0.8	4.5 0.7	3.9 0.7
Total Battery	4.3 1.2	3.9 1.2	4.6 1.1	4.7 1.2	3.7 1.0	4.3 1.3	3.4 1.0	5.0 1.1	3.9 0.9

Table 2

Fifth Grade Students' Grade Equivalency Scores, Means and Standard Deviations:
by Sex, Race, and Sex X Race

	All Ss (N111)	Sex		Race		White - Black Male		White - Black Female	
		M (N49)	F (N62)	W (N63)	B (N48)	WM (N30)	BM (N19)	WF (N32)	BF (N30)
R-VOC	6.2 1.7	6.1 1.8	6.2 1.6	6.6 1.6	5.6 1.7	6.6 1.8	5.4 1.6	6.6 1.4	5.8 1.9
R-CM	6.7 2.3	6.5 2.1	6.9 2.4	7.3 2.1	6.1 2.3	7.0 2.0	5.7 2.1	7.5 2.2	6.3 2.4
R-TL	6.4 1.8	6.2 1.7	6.5 2.0	6.9 1.6	5.9 2.0	6.7 1.6	5.5 1.6	7.1 1.7	6.1 2.2
Spelling	7.4 3.0	7.5 3.1	7.3 2.9	7.6 2.8	7.2 3.2	7.4 3.0	7.8 3.3	7.8 2.6	6.8 3.1
L-WC	8.1 2.8	7.6 2.6	8.6 2.9	8.7 2.5	7.4 3.0	7.8 2.2	7.3 3.2	9.5 2.5	7.4 2.9
L-EX	7.0 2.6	6.7 2.7	7.3 2.5	7.8 2.7	6.0 2.2	7.5 2.9	5.4 1.9	8.1 2.4	6.3 2.3
L-TL	7.5 2.5	7.1 2.5	7.8 2.5	8.2 2.4	6.5 2.4	7.6 2.5	6.2 2.4	8.7 2.2	6.7 2.5
M-CM	6.5 1.3	6.2 1.2	6.6 1.3	6.6 1.3	6.3 1.2	6.1 1.1	6.4 1.3	7.1 1.2	6.1 1.2
M-CN	6.1 1.4	6.1 1.5	6.0 1.3	6.5 1.3	5.5 1.3	6.3 1.5	5.8 1.7	6.6 1.2	5.3 1.1
M-Total	6.2 1.2	6.2 1.1	6.3 1.2	6.5 1.1	5.9 1.2	6.2 0.9	6.1 1.4	6.8 1.1	5.7 1.0
Total Battery	6.4 1.4	6.2 1.3	6.5 1.5	6.7 1.3	5.9 1.4	6.3 1.1	6.0 1.5	7.1 1.4	5.9 1.4

Table 3

Tenth Grade Students' Grade Equivalency Scores, Means and Standard Deviations:
by Sex, Race, and Sex X Race

	All Ss (N609)	Sex M (N296)	F (N313)	Race W (N361)	B (N248)	White – Black Male WM (N171)	BM (N125)	White – Black Female WF (N190)	BF (N123)
R-VOC	10.1 2.5	9.9 2.6	10.3 2.5	11.0 2.1	8.7 2.5	10.8 2.3	8.7 2.5	11.2 1.8	8.8 2.6
R-CN	10.3 2.7	10.2 2.8	10.5 2.6	11.3 2.2	9.0 2.7	11.0 2.5	9.0 2.7	11.4 2.0	9.0 2.7
R-TL	10.3 2.5	10.9 2.5	10.5 2.4	11.2 2.0	8.9 2.5	11.0 2.2	8.9 2.4	11.4 1.8	9.0 2.5
Spelling	10.3 2.8	9.6 2.9	10.9 2.4	10.6 2.5	9.8 3.0	10.0 2.8	9.1 3.0	11.2 2.0	10.5 2.8
L-MC	10.4 2.9	9.9 3.2	10.9 2.6	11.5 2.3	8.9 3.0	11.0 2.6	8.4 3.3	12.0 1.9	9.4 2.7
L-EX	10.7 2.7	10.3 2.9	11.0 2.4	11.5 2.2	9.5 2.9	11.1 2.6	9.3 3.0	11.8 1.8	9.8 2.8
L-TL	10.7 2.6	10.3 2.9	11.1 2.3	11.6 2.0	9.4 2.8	11.2 2.4	9.0 3.0	12.0 1.6	9.7 2.6
M-CM	11.0 1.9	10.8 2.1	11.2 1.8	11.5 1.6	10.3 2.2	11.3 1.8	10.2 2.3	11.7 1.4	10.3 2.0
M-CN	10.6 2.3	10.5 2.4	10.7 2.1	11.3 1.9	9.6 2.3	11.2 2.1	9.6 2.5	11.4 1.8	9.5 2.1
M-TL	10.8 2.0	10.6 2.1	10.9 1.8	11.4 1.6	9.9 2.1	11.2 1.8	9.9 2.2	11.6 1.4	9.9 1.9
Total Battery	10.5 2.3	10.2 2.4	10.7 2.1	11.4 1.9	9.5 2.3	11.1 2.1	9.2 2.4	11.7 1.5	9.7 2.2

ment of the rate of academic progress of minority and "less advanced" students, without material detriment to whites. (4)

School desegregation has been the law of the land for more than a generation and it is now possible to appraise the limited available data concerning desegregatory achievement effects. The· results have not affirmed certain expectations of the judiciary and the NAACP. In *Debra P. vs Turlington,* the NAACP originally emphasized ethnic disparities on test scores and argued that literacy tests unfairly penalized black students because they had not received an integrated education. U.S. District Court Judge George Carr therefore ordered a four year delay in implementing literacy tests as a criterion for graduation until all vestiges of school desegregation were gone. Four years later, blacks constituted only 21% of the state's high school population but 62% of those who failed. The NAACP sought a continued ban on withholding diplomas for those who failed the state's functional literacy tests. This Carr denied, because the students had attended a desegregated high school and racial disparities could not therefore be attributed to segregated education. (5)

Throughout the nation, major school districts continue to expand busing programs on the assumption that black children learn more effectively when schools are racially balanced. (6) Actual studies, however, fail to establish a clear linkage between forced busing and higher black achievement levels; as courts seek to shape appropriate remedies they experience a perplexing division of expert opinion. In the early 1980s, the National Institute of Education conducted an extensive investigation into busing effects. The result: the nation's top researchers, while disagreeing on the desegregation achievement question, were unable to identify a single longitudinal study which demonstrated that busing enhances black learning. (7)

Additionally, individual scholars have arrived at differing conclusions regarding desegregatory effects. Hawley has declared

(4)   McMillan, James B. *Hearings before the Subcommittee on Separation of Powers of the Committee on the Judiciary, United States Senate,* October 16, 1981, 511-582.

(5)   *Debra P. vs. Turlington, 474 F. Supp. 244 (M.D. Fla. 1979; Aff'd in part and vacated and remanded, 644 F2d 397 (5th Cir. 1981).*

(6)   Tomorrow: A look ahead from the nation's capital. *U.S. News & World Report,* April 14, 1986, p. 29.

(7)   Uribe, O. *The Effects of School Desegregation on the Academic Achievement of Black Students.* Washington, D.C.: National Institute of Education, September 1983.

that busing raises black learning levels, but in support of this cites only short term studies, which have produced inconsistent findings. (8) Grant and Sleeter have argued that the educational literature treats race, social class and gender as separate issues. They state that this oversimplifies appraisals of student school behaviors, and serves to perpetuate gender, class and race bias. (9)

Pursuing the Grant-Sleeter hypotheses, Scott analyzed profiles of tenth grade students who had never attended segregated schools. (10) Comparing gender and race achievement profiles, he found that whites obtained significantly higher scores in all achievement areas. However, the ethnic gap varied by achievement area, with narrowest ethnic gaps in Spelling and Mathematics Computation and the widest gap in Reading. Within-race differentials also appeared. Black males outperformed black females in Reading and Language (Expression), whereas black females scored higher than black males in Spelling and Language (Mechanics). The within-race achievement gaps of whites were narrower than those of blacks; white females outperformed white males in Spelling and Language (Mechanics), whereas white males scored higher than white females in Math (Concepts and Applications). From these data Scott suggested the possible merit of assessing individual students' profiles, as one strategy to more effectively individualize learning strategies. The present study is designed to provide additional and replicative data concerning sex and race learning profiles within a desegregated school setting.

Method: Within a metropolitan and southern school district which had been desegregated for more than 15 years, *California Achievement Test (CAT)* scores were obtained on all third and fifth grade students in three elementary schools and on tenth grade students in a large high school. The local administration considered the student population of the target schools representative of the district as a whole. The school district serves a large geographic area which has grown in population and

(8)   Hawley, Willis D. False premises, false promises: The mythical character of public discourse about education. *Phi Delta Kappan,* November 1985, 183-187.
(9)   Grant, Carl A. and Sleeter, Christine E. Race, Class and Gender in Educational Research: An Argument for Integrative Analysis. *Review of Educational Research,* Summer 1986, Vol. 56 (2), 195-211.
(10)   Scott, Ralph S. Race Sex and race achievement profiles in a desegregated high school in the deep South. *Mankind Quarterly,* Spring 1985, Vol. 25 (3), 291-302.

affluence during the past several decades and is of mixed rural and urban character. School officials identified the sex and race of each student. Group administration of the *CAT* was conducted, and scores obtained on the following test measures: Reading (Vocabulary), Reading (Comprehension), Reading (Total), Spelling, Language (Mechanics), Language (Expression), Language (Total), Math (Computation), Math (Concepts and Applications), Math (Total), and Total Battery. No student enrolled in special educational programming was included in the study.

The sampling consisted of 107 third graders (20 black males, 20 black females, 28 white males, 39 white females); 111 fifth graders (19 black males, 30 black females, 30 white males, 32 white females) and 608 tenth graders (126 black males, 124 black females, 169 white males, 189 white females). On each of the *CAT* subtests, as well as for the Total Battery, means and standard deviations were obtained for all subjects by sex and by race, and also race x sex. Analysis of variance was employed to appraise the extent of variance attributable to sex, to race, and to interaction of race and sex.

Results: Tables 1 through 3 summarize results at the three grade levels. These tables present the average grade equivalency for identified subjects (all Subjects, Male, Female, White, Black) in the top left of each cell, with the standard deviations just below and in the lower right. Various achievement measures on the *CAT* are identified in the far left column. These tables show that at the third and fifth grade levels the average for the total sample was above presumed national norms on all 22 achievement areas tested. At the tenth grade level this trend was reversed, with the subjects scoring below the presumed national average on 9 of 11 measurements. The elevated scores at the lower levels are of considerable magnitude. For example, the Spelling average for third graders was 5.6. Since testing took place in April, national norms for this sample would be expected to approximate 3.8 (third grade and eighth month), but on Spelling the students of this third grade sample scored 1.8 grade levels higher than general expectancy. On third grade Spelling, white and black averages exceeded national norms by 2.3 and 1.0 grade levels respectively. Similarly, elevated scores are noted at the fifth grade level. In Language (MC) the fifth graders averaged 8.1 or 2.3 grade levels above approximated national norms, black and white averages surpassed presumed national norms by 2.9 and 1.6 grade levels respectively. With tenth graders there is no elevation in test scores and averages are slightly below national expectancies (10.5, expectancy of 10.8). However, white tenth graders scored above national expectancy on all subtests except Spelling. The white average on this (Spelling) subtest is .1 below presumed national norms, however, white females scored .4 above, but white males .8 below, the hypothetical national average of 10.8.

These tables also demonstrate that females in general obtained higher scores than their male counterparts. Thus females' scores were higher on all 11 measures at the third grade level, 9 of 11 measures at fifth grade, and 10 of 11 at tenth grade. The magnitude of gender differences varied considerably. Third grade findings show that the smallest sex achievement gap was .3 of a grade level in Math (CM), and the largest in Spelling and Language (MC), where the differential was 1.3.

Tables 1 to 3 also show that at the third grade level white females secured higher achievement scores than white males, and that the differential equaled or exceeded a full grade level in Spelling and all three Language measures. Likewise, third grade black females secured higher scores than black males on all 11 measures, and in all three Language measures the gap exceeded a full grade level. At the fifth grade white females obtained higher achievement scores than white males on 10 measures, and in Reading (Voc) there were no within-race differences. In two academic areas, Language (MC) and Language (Total) the gaps exceeded a grade level and in Math (CM) the gap was one grade unit. The attainments of fifth grade black females exceeded those of black fifth grade males on six measures; black males obtained higher scores than black females on all three Math measures and on Total Battery. Black fifth grade males' Spelling norm was a full grade level higher than that of black females. Finally, tenth grade white females outperformed white males in all 11 achievement areas tested and their attainments were at least a full grade level higher in the two areas, Spelling and Language (MC). Tenth grade black females obtained higher scores than black males in eight measures and on two of them, Reading (CN) and Math (Total), tenth grade black males and females secured identical scores. On two measures, Spelling and Language (MC), the differences were at least a full grade level.

Tables 1 through 3 also demonstrate that whites obtained

Table 4

Analysis of Variance of Third Grade Black and White Students
by Sex, by Race, and by Sex X Race

	Main Effects	Sex	Race	Interactions, Race X Sex
R-VC	40.3 .00	2.6 .16	36.3 .00	.22 .90
R-CN	50.1 .00	4.5 .08	43.7 .00	.81 .45
R-TL	69.8 .00	5.3 .09	70.0 .00	.03 .90
Spelling	64.5 .01	26.2 .05	33.3 .03	7.3 .29
L-MC	54.7 .00	35.4 .00	15.3 .04	.72 .65
L-EX	70.7 .00	30.4 .00	34.7 .00	.01 .94
L-TL	88.2 .00	45.8 .00	35.6 .00	.41 .72
M-CH	6.1 .00	1.9 .05	3.7 .00	.00 .98
M-CN	22.3 .00	4.6 .04	16.2 .00	.13 .73
M-TL	12.3 .00	3.2 .03	8.2 .00	.00 .92
Total Battery	26.5 .00	7.6 .01	18.6 .00'	.22 .67

all 33 achievement comparisons: 11 at each of the third, fifth and tenth grade levels. In virtually all comparisons the ethnic differences are substantially higher than those noted with respect to gender. For example, third grade white females outperformed white males in Reading (Total) by half grade level (.5), and black females secured scores .4 higher than black males on this measure; the ethnic difference on this measure was 1.6 grade equivalences. White males and females both scored approximately a grade and a half higher than their black gender counterparts.

Tables 4 through 6 summarize analysis of variance findings. On these tables, and within each cell, the Sum of Squares is listed in the top left, and the statistical significance in the lower right. For example, and in appraising gender effects for third grade students in Language (MC), the Sum of Squares was 35.4 and the (gender) differences are significant at the .00 level. Table 4 shows that, at least at the .05 level of significance and with third graders, statistically significant gender differences occured in Spelling and on the three Language, the three Math and the Total Battery measures. An examination of Table 1 shows that the significant Spelling differences are associated with gender and race profiles, but that the latter contributed more significantly to the obtained finding of statistical significance. Thus on Spelling, third grade white females outscored white males by 1.5 grade levels, whereas black females outdistanced black males by .4; white females' scores were 1.7 higher than those of black females, while scores of white males were .6 higher than those of black males.

Ethnic differences are also apparent on Table 4; these are not surprising since Table 1 reveals that third grade whites secured significantly higher attainments than blacks on all 11 measures. Table 4 shows that ethnic differentials are apparently much greater in some areas than others; for example, the Sum of Squares associated with race on Reading (Total) is 70.0 but only 3.7 in Math (CM).

At the fifth grade level, and as shown on Table 5, there were no statistically significant gender differences. This table also reveals that significant race differences were found on all subtests except Spelling and M-CM. Reference to Table 2 suggests that elevated and a skewed norming distribution probably explains these two findings of fifth grade non-statistical signifi-

Table 5

Analysis of Variance of Fifth Grade Black and White Students
by Sex, by Race, and by Sex X Race

	Main Effects	Sex	Race	Interactions, Race X Sex
R-VC	26.6 .01	1.4 .48	26.3 .00	1.4 .49
R-CN	46.2 .01	8.8 .18	41.1 .00	0.4 .93
R-TL	35.1 .01	8.2 .12	30.0 .00	.22 .80
Spelling	4.9 .76	2.2 .62	2.2 .62	14.7 .20
L-MC	63.1 .02	24.0 .08	45.3 .01	17.6 .12
L-EX	110.5 .00	15.1 .12	102.0 .00	.59 .76
L-TL	82.0 .00	17.4 .09	71.0 .00	2.5 .51
M-CM	5.3 .18	3.1 .16	2.7 .19	9.7 .01
M-CN	23.2 .00	0.3 .67	22.2 .00	3.6 .15
M-TL	9.1 .03	.32 .61	9.06 .00	7.03 .02
Total Battery	15.3 .02	3.1 .19	13.1 .01	4.0 .14

cance; white Spelling scores averaged 1.8 grade level above the assumed national average of 5.8, and the black average was 1.4 above this hypothesized national mean. Considerable variability appears with respect to the ethnic achievement gap at fifth grade, the largest in Language (EX) of 1.8 grade equivalence, the narrowest in Math (CM) of .3. Within-race sex differences were also apparent. On Language (MC), white males outscored black males by .5 of a grade level whereas white females averaged 2.1 grade levels higher than black females.

Analysis of variance concerning tenth graders of this study are summarized on Table 6. Here significant sex differences appear in Spelling, the three Language measures and Total Battery. Reference to Table 3 indicates that these significant gender differences are substantially attributable to the higher scores of whites with respect to the attainments of their same-gender blacks. In Spelling, white males scored .9 higher than black males whereas white females' scores were .7 above those of black females; also, white females scored 1.2 higher than white males and black females 1.4 grade units higher than black males. Also, wide differences are noted in magnitude of the ethnic differences, the widest tenth grade ethnic gap on Language(MC) 2.6 grade units, and the narrowest in Spelling (.8). The gap, however, increases when gender-race comparisons are drawn. Here the widest achievement gap between white females and black males was in Language (MC) where the differential was 3.6 grade units.

Discussion: The findings of this study provide replicative support for a number of conclusions reached in an earlier research study of tenth grade students, conducted by this investigator.(11) In that study, the scores of students who had always attended desegregated schools revealed consistent and large ethnic differences, and smaller and less consistent gender effects. On all measures, whites secured significantly higher scores than blacks; females generally attained higher scores than males but the gender gap was significantly narrower, and prevailed in fewer achievement areas than observed with respect to ethnicity. In the present investigation, no significant gender differences appear in any of the Reading measures, but significant differences are observed in Spelling (third and tenth grade), all three Language measures (third and tenth grade)

(11)   Scott, op. cit.

Table 6

Analysis of Variance of Tenth Grade Black and White Students
by Sex, by Race, and by Sex X Race

	Main Effects	Sex	Race	Interactions, Race X Sex
R-VC	762.3 .00	11.7 .13	745.1 .00	5.5 .30
R-CN	773.6 .00	6.8 .29	762.1 .00	5.7 .34
R-TL	780.3 .00	11.7 .12	762.6 .00	5.7 .28
Spelling	349.2 .00	243.9 .00	96.5 .00	1.6 .63
L-MC	1140.1 .00	132.9 .00	986.2 .00	0.0 .95
L-EX	616.1 .00	52.9 .00	552.8 .00	1.2 .67
L-TL	818.1 .00	76.1 .00	728.3 .00	0.0 .93
M-CN	237.3 .00	9.8 .09	224.6 .00	5.1 .22
M-CN	424.6 .00	1.2 .60	421.6 .00	5.1 .28
M-TL	309.3 .00	3.7 .29	303.1 .00	7.3 .14
Total Battery	329.3 .00	26.2 .01	306.8 .00	0.2 .82

and all three Math areas (third grade). Statistically significant ethnic differences, with whites obtaining the higher scores, are noted on all 11 measures of the *CAT* (third and tenth grade) and 9 of 11 measures (fifth grade).

The results of this study lead to five general observations. First, achievement scores yielded by the *CAT* appear to be inflated. When, for example, the average score from a sampling of white fifth graders exceeds presumed national norms by almost three grade levels [as is the case of Language (Mechanics)], it is doubtful that test scores can be taken seriously. Further research may demonstrate that some school administrators are tempted to use tests which produce elevated scores. There are obvious political advantages in public announcements that students in a given school district score higher under desegregated schooling conditions. However, any such political use of inflated test scores is likely to prove ultimately counterproductive. Actual achievement, and not misleading high scores, is positively correlated with authentic student competencies and later employability. In fact, inflated scores may lead to a false sense of security with respect to educational efficacy, a complacency not justified on the basis of recent evidence that black unemployment and illiteracy levels have risen during the past several decades. (12, 13)

Secondly, the one exception to test score elevation involves tenth grade profiles; this is a surprising development since the author's previous investigation revealed that *CAT* tenth grade scores were extremely elevated. (14) Since the tenth grade students in the present study had always attended desegregated schools, replication studies seem warranted to ascertain, as some researchers suggest, whether the dynamics associated with desegregation (or forced busing) tend to increase the incidence of student alienation, especially with disadvantaged students who fail to achieve a modicum of academic success. (15, 16)

A third observation is that the findings consistently show that black achievements fall significantly below those of whites,

(12)   Jacob, J.E. Education: The Key to Economic Survival. *Vital Speeches of the Day*, Vol. 52, 229-231, 1986.

(13)   Veder, Richard and Gallaway, Lowell. AFDC and the Laffer Principle, *Wall Street Journal*, March 26, 1986.

(14)   Scott, op. cit.

(15)   Newmann, Fred M. Reducing Student Alienation. *Harvard Educational Review*, November 1981, Vol. 51 (4), 546-563.

(16)   Fisher, Sethard. Race, class, anomie and academic achievement. *Urban*

although the school district has been desegregated since the students entered kindergarten. This finding suggests that widely held views concerning desegregatory achievement effects, still popularly held in some judicial and academic circles, require more extensive investigation which should consider the impact of home background factors on student learning profiles. The data of this study, for example, reveal that despite elevated scores which resulted in many students securing maxium scores which severed the usually long upper tail of the skewed curve far below its usual placement in the normal "bell shaped" curve, the black-white achievement gap equaled or exceeded a standard deviation on most measures. It therefore appears that, on measures which yield a normal distribution of test scores, the ethnic differences would be substantially greater than those reported on the *CAT*.

The character of gender differences constitutes a fourth observation. At all three grade levels females, both black and white, generally obtained higher scores than their same-gender and race counterparts, a finding which merits further investigation.

Finally, results of this experiment support earlier research conducted by Scott(17) as well as Grant and Sleeter,(18) which indicates that race, social class and gender must be treated as separate but interrelated factors. Granted that class factors are difficult to control experimentally, it appears inappropriate for researchers to ignore the important interaction of gender and race. If the goal of education is to provide each student with quality instruction it would seem that gender-race trends should be utilized since they provide useful guidelines for enhancing prospects that each student be provided with appropriate and at least quasi-individualized learning experiences.

Education, Vol. 16 (2), July 1981, 149-174.
   (17)   Scott, op. cit.
   (18)   Grant and Sleeter, op. cit.

DESEGREGATORY EFFECTS IN
CHARLOTTE-MECKLENBURG COUNTY SCHOOLS LONGITUDINAL DEMOGRAPHICS ON BLACK ACHIEVEMENT AND MIDDLE CLASS FLIGHT

A case history of the results of court-ordered racial integration in Charlotte-Mecklenburg County schools reveals no improvement in academic competency of minority students, despite the high financial cost and the disruption of student stability profiles.

This paper focuses on appraisal of desegregatory* effects within the schools of Charlotte-Mecklenburg County (C-MC) North Carolina, with respect to black achievement and middle class flight. The C-MC school district, as a result of *Swann vs. Charlotte-Mecklenburg Board of Education,* (1) has served as the national prototype of metropolitan desegregation, and therefore it should be possible to obtain, by appraising longitudinal data in C-MC, a comprehensive understanding of long-term desegregatory consequences on black achievement and student stability. Desegregatory effects in these two areas are particularly relevant, inasmuch as it is difficult to justify mandated busing of children from their neighborhood schools if the practice either fails to promote black learning, or if it accelerates the flight of middle class families from the public schools. If in fact mandated desegregation increases middle class flight, then a different segregated population has been created. Such resegregation would leave public schools to essentially serve those poor and minority youth whose parents cannot afford to resettle in another disctrict or to send their children to a private school.

Chances of desegregatory success in C-MC were not merely random; in many respects they were optimum. Professor Finger who designed the C-MC plan observed that his busing plan

---

* Throughout this paper, the terms "desegregation" and "busing" are considered synonyms, indicating circumstances wherein parents are required to send their children to non-neighborhood schools. The term "integration" refers to circumstances in which parents enjoy the choice of sending their children to a neighborhood school or to a non-neighborhood school, and, voluntarily elect the latter.

(1) *Swann vs. Charlotte-Mecklenburg County,* 306 F. Supp. 1291.

possessed a number of geographic advantages. (2) C-MC is about 40 miles long and 20 miles wide, and Charlotte is centrally located within the county. So one could not easily work in Charlotte and live outside the school district: the "catchment areas" were not only large but also free of problems which might have been initiated had the city of Charlotte been on the fringe of the school district. Since implementation of the C-MC plan, Finger has claimed that C-MC integration is successful not only because white flight was difficult, but because the court took immediate corrective action whenever one area changed in its population, therefore assuring built-in safeguards for residential stability.

Background of Swann

Litigation concerning C-MC was not isolated. *Swann* was issued barely a year after the Supreme Court, ruling in *Green vs. County School Board of New Kent County*, had rejected "freedom of choice" plans in favor of more immediate efforts to desegregate. In *Green*, Justice William Brennan had written for a unanimous court that "the burden of a school board today is to come forward with a plan that promises realistically to work, and promises realistically to work now."

By "working," the Supreme Court apparently meant racial balancing of public schools, even if this meant denying black and white parents the option of having their children attend a neighborhood school. Racial balance, however desired or undesired by parents, was to be the law of the land, at least in southern schools which had initially been segregated by law (*de jure* segregation), as opposed to northern-style segregation — by housing and schools — based not on law but on presumably normal social circumstances (*de facto* segregation).

An historical review of C-MC litigation reveals that, prior to

(2)   Finger, John A. "Why busing plans work." *School Review*, May 1976, pp. 364-372; the significance of *Swann* to cities wherein circumstances may be less optimal than those described for C-MC is emphasized in *The Swann vs. Charlotte-Mecklenburg Case*: Its significance for Tennessee Schools, *Tennessee Education*; 1 (4), pp. 8-15, May 1972. Behind the *Swann* case is the unsettled question whether neighborhood schools need be violated once a *de jure* segregated system is declared racially integrated. As former Chief Justice Potter Stewart remarked on June 10, 1981 (*Washington Post*, June 11, 1981), "(Brown) simply held that it was unconstitutional to keep children out of a public tax-supported school based upon the color of the skin. It didn't say anything about there having to be in every school building a proportion of white and non-white students and so on..."

Swann, vestiges of *de jure* segregation were being voluntarily corrected. C-MC schools were consolidated in July 1960. At that time, more than two thirds of the black students attended totally black schools: over 90% of black students resided in the inner city of an area less than 10% of the geographic area of the county. However, the district, since the early 1960s, had implemented long-range policies aimed at color-blind attendance policies, in which school attendance was based on residence. In 1965-66, some former county schools were closed. From 1964 to 1969, the number of black students attending integrated schools had increased from a few dozen to nearly 10,000. Black students attended all but 8 of the 106 schools, and attendance at those eight schools (5,514) constituted only a small fraction of the C-MC student population.

When *Swann* was decreed, the C-MC district covered 550 square miles, comprised 106 schools and served 84,000 students, grades 1-12. In this combined city-county district, whites constituted 71%, and blacks 29%, of the student population. School attendance was determined by residence and freedom-of-choice transfer provisions for minority students; the county-wide area transported 22,157 pupils in 250 buses at a total cost of $666,348.03.

In *Swann,* Judge James B. McMillan ordered the C-MC district to undertake substantial busing by grouping schools into clusters and by balancing most schools of the system. The first order called for black ratios in the schools from 3 to 41%. School officials appealed and were upheld by the Fourth Circuit Court of Appeals which declared Judge McMillan's decision "overly harsh." However, the Supreme Court overruled the Fourth Circuit.

Writing for the high court's unanimous decision, Chief Justice Warren Burger declared that when local officials defaulted in their obligation to end *de jure* segregation, the Fourteenth Amendment's equal protection clause gave wide latitude to federal courts seeking remedy. Racial balancing was therefore upheld, as long as busing was not dangerous to students or harmful to their education. While upholding metro-busing, however, the high court established important qualifications. Every school need not be racially balanced; a small number of essentially one-race schools was permissible if it were established that such enrollments reflected "genuinely non-discrimination" assignments. One proof of such procedures would be a transfer policy permitting blacks access to largely white schools.* The Court also recognized that resegregation, based on what was then spoken of as "white flight," might occur. On this the Court concluded that "neither school authorities nor federal district courts are constitutionally required to make year-by-year adjustments of student bodies once the affirmative duty to desegregate has been accomplished and racial discrimination through official action (*de jure*) is eliminated from the system." Apparently the court intended, once and for all, to uproot vestiges of *de jure* segregation in C-MC, after which the district presumably could serve children on the basis of color-blind policies.

Charlotte-Meckleburg Today

In the fall of 1984, the C-MC school system was the 30th largest system in the U.S. with 71,925 students in grades K-12. The student population was 61% white, 39% black, and was composed of 108 schools of which 75 were elementary, 22 junior, and 11 senior highs. In 1981, the school system transported 48,000 students. Of these, school officials state that approximately 12,000 were bused for purposes of racial balance, at an estimated annual cost of $4 million. In C-MC, busing is essentially a bi-ethnic matter. There are few non-black minority students, although the Asian population has shown a remarkable percentile growth. Thus in 1979-80, minority students in C-MC were: Indian .4%, Asian .7%, and Hispanic .3%; in the fall of 1982 comparable figures were .5%, 1.3%, and .4%.

Claims Regarding Schooling Benefits of Mandated Desegregation

After more than a decade of C-MC busing, there are those who assert that the practice has brought about a higher level of schooling. Superintendent Jay M. Robinson states that the overall quality of education in the county system is better now

---

* It was judicially established in *Moore vs. Charlotte-Mecklenburg Board of Education* (Supreme Court of the United States, October term, 1970, #444), that each year any pupil was at liberty to request assignment to another school; that "no reason for transfer need be given"; and that "all transfer requests are honored," unless the school to which the transfer is requested is full. (p. 438)

than it would have been without *Swann*. (3) Says Robinson: "Achievement scores and behavior are improved, while parent and community support is strong and race relations have likewise improved." Similar sentiments are echoed by Judge McMillan. (4)

The present study is designed to appraise — drawing upon primary statistical facts as much as possible, since the subject is highly emotional — varying effects of metro-wide mandated desegregation on the schooling process. If busing is to be continued, it seems reasonable to require evidence that the practice has promoted, and promotes, the quality of education, especially for black students for whom mandated desegregation was undertaken as a "remedy." But has desegregation improved the quality of education provided black youth? A study of schooling effects should help clarify just what, if anything, busing does to promote educational equity for minority youth.

II. Schooling Effects

In *Swann,* Judge McMillan quoted one of the attorneys at the first hearing in a discussion about reassignments and school buses: "The question is really not one of busing, but whether what the child gets when he gets off the bus is worth the trouble." In this study, educational outcomes of busing are examined in two broad categories: achievement, and student stability. The latter is sometimes referred to as white flight but the writer designates the phenomenon as middle class flight since parents of all races have reportedly taken steps to avoid mandated desegregation for their children. (5)

A. Achievement Outcomes:
Does Busing Promote Black Learning?

In some respects, achievement is the most easily measured of

(3)   Robinson, Jay. *Hearings before the Subcommittee on Separation of Powers of the Committee on the Judiciary, United States Senate, Serial No. J-97-29,* May 22, September 30, October 1 and 16, 1981; see especially pp. 564-565. Also, see *Education Daily,* September 18, 1981.

(4)   *Hearings befor the Subcommittee on Separation of Powers,* op. cit., p. 511+.

(5)   Gerard, H.B. and Miller, N. *School Desegregation:* New York: Plenum, 1975; see also, Gerard, H.B. School desegregation: The social science role. *American Psychologist,* 38, 869-877. Also, see Scott, R.S. Remedial options and alternatives with respect to a metropolitan school desegregation plan. Paper prepared for the Office of the Attorney General, State of Missouri, 1982.

schooling effects. The question of achievement outcomes weighed heavily in Judge McMillan's 1969 ruling. In *Swann*, (6) McMillan concluded that segregation produces inferior education because, under segregated conditions, the average black learning level was substantially below that of whites. This differential, McMillan claimed, "cannot be explained solely in terms of cultural, racial, or family background without honestly facing the impact of segregation." In making this statement, however, McMillan provided neither statistics concerning home background factors nor data on learning levels of black and white children *before* they entered school. In McMillan's judgment, racial integration of the public schools was substantially based on evidence that a significant racial achievement gap existed, and would be "remedied" or narrowed by desegregation.

McMillan referred to the "uncontradicted testimony of the experts and administrators (who) all agreed that transferring underprivileged black children from black schools into schools with 70% or more white students produced a dramatic improvement in the rate of (academic) progress and an increase in the absolute performance of the less advanced students, without material deteriment to whites. There was no contrary evidence."(7) He added that segregation would, however, be illegal even if racial integration did not promote achievement.

In establishing the "desegregation-higher black achievement" thesis, McMillan inserted a statistical table into the *Swann* record which summarized black and white achievement scores. Respective black and white grade equivalence scores for C-MC during 1968-69, were as follows: Spelling 4.3 and 6.6 (4.3 representing average black skills at the competency level of fourth grade third month); Language 3.6 and 6.9; Math 3.9 and 5.5; and Word Meaning 4.0 and 6.2. McMillan assumed that a large proportion of the racial achievement differences could be attributed to schooling effects.

McMillan also referred to the tendency for the black-white

(6)   *Swann,* op. cit.
(7)   *Hearings,* op. cit., especially p. 534; here McMillan reiterates his basis for concluding, in *Swann,* that claims concerning desegregatory achievement benefits are uncontradicted, which implies that the issue is not debatable since the evidence is overwhelming.
*   In the fall of 1982, only 17 of C-MC's 108 schools met the criterion of 70% or more white students.

achievement gap to widen the longer C-MC students attended segregated schools. But this is simply a manifestation of the "Progressive Achievement Decrement "(PAD), which is observed in any (group) comparison of environmentally advantaged children. Actually, it would be unnatural if PAD did not occur. For example, when a poor and experientially disadvantaged child, irrespective of race, enters kindergarten at five years of age with a 20% deficit in (average) learning, the mental age of the child (the concept of mental age introduces statistical problems, but the problem is complex and let us be tolerant of issues which, while relevant, are not of practical significance) would not be five years (60 months) but rather 80% of that (48 months). With a tenth grade child, the mental age in absolute terms would be higher (16 years, or 192 months) and the 20% gap then is approximately 38.4 months but still of the same estimated magnitude (20%) as observed when the child entered school.

In his ruling, McMillan presented no information concerning family background or the segregated students' performance upon entry into kindergarten; instead he referred only to the consequence of PAD in observing the sixth grade difference. However, his findings of fact — that the racial achievement gap could be significantly ascribed to school segregation, that black children experienced greater difficulty the longer they were in segregated schools, and that racial balancing of the schools would improve minority achievement — were affirmed by the Fourth Circuit Court of Appeals and the U.S. Supreme Court.

McMillan's position in 1981, given before a U.S. Senate Subcommittee, is that the racial achievement gap has significantly diminished since the onset of Charlotte-Mecklenburg busing: "...Accomplishments of C-MC students for the first time are better in many ways than the national average...Performance of Charlotte-Mecklenburg students has been going up for the past 4 or 5 years, where, nationally, we are told, performance is going down."(8) The Subcommittee was given a similarly upbeat view by Superintendent Jay M. Robinson.

But it is uncertain whether these optimistic reports are entirely accurate. In 1979, the district released test scores. At that time, 43% of black 11th graders failed to pass a test on

(8)   Ibid.

basic reading and math; 29% failed the reading section of the test and 38% failed the math section. (9) For whites, the failure percentages were 3% and 4% respectively. Statewide in North Carolina, 25% of blacks failed the reading test and 34% failed math; for whites the figures were 4% and 5%. Superintendent Robinson lamented that other school districts held special sessions for 11th graders who felt they could not pass the test, but this was not possible in C-MC because "test-teaching" would cause resegregation. Robinson pledged to raise Charlotte-Mecklenburg scores and did not exclude the option of finding justifiable ways to "test-teach" in C-MC, through procedures which would raise test scores but not create racial imbalances within and between instructional groupings of students.

What Do Achievement Test Scores Signify?

In the fall of 1977, C-MC began using the *California Achievement Test (CAT)*, which replaced the *Stanford Achievement Test (SAT)*. The *CAT* makes available, to teachers across the country, a *"Classroom Management Guide"* that contains, says one educational researcher, "...a plethora of *CAT*-related eductional activities" (10) which may be given students prior to testing.

In recent years, C-MC students have attained higher scores on the *CAT* than they did on the *SAT*, although it is uncertain if they were "test-taught." For example, Table 1 shows that average C-MC 6th grade Reading Comprehension scores (in grade equivalences) were 5.8 in 1968, 5.6 in 1974, and 7.8 in 1981; a two year gain is obviously significant. On Table 2, similar trends are observed in math.

If student learning levels are truly enhanced, then higher scores should not be limited to the *CAT* but should also be observed on non-*CAT* achievement measures. But this apparently hasn't occurred in C-MC. On the *Scholastic Aptitude Test,* the Verbal score was 422 in 1974 and 403 in 1982; the Math *SAT* was 455 in 1974, 440 in 1982. Relative to North Carolina schools generally, Table 3 shows that C-MC attainments have fallen off. This may be related to such factors as middle class flight but, if so, another basis arises for examining the educa-

(9)   *Charlotte Observor,* January 1979.

(10)   Schell, Leo M. Test review of the *California Achievement Test: Reading Forms C and D, Journal of Reading,* April 1980, pp. 624-628.

Table 1

CHARLOTTE-MECKLENBURG SCHOOLS
Longitudinal Report of Achievement Test Data
READING COMPREHENSION
Grades 3 and 6

Chart A

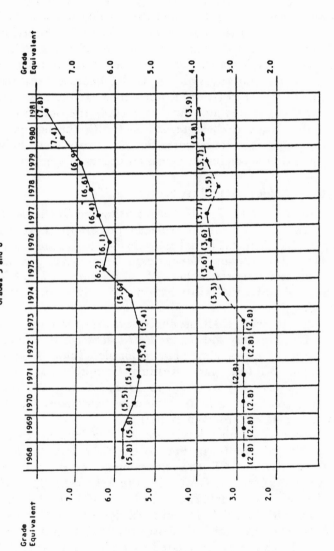

Code: 3rd Grade ---------- National Norm 3.7
       6th Grade ———————— National Norm 6.7

Table 2

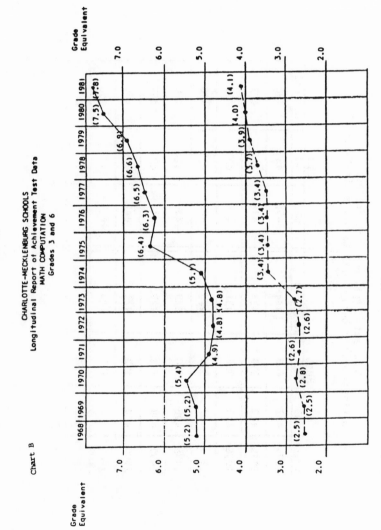

Chart B

CHARLOTTE-MECKLENBURG SCHOOLS
Longitudinal Report of Achievement Test Data
MATH COMPUTATION
Grades 3 and 6

Code: 3rd Grade --------- National Norm 3.7
      6th Grade ————————— National Norm 6.7

Table 3

Scholastic Aptitude Test Scores:
Charlotte-Mecklenburg, North Carolina and National
1974-82

Year	VERBAL			MATH		
	CMS	NC	National	CMS	NC	National
1974	422	409	444	455	437	480
1975	417	399	434	446	428	472
1976	410	396	431	439	423	472
1977	409	394	429	442	425	470
1978	405	390	429	436	424	468
1979	409	393	427	444	426	467
1980	404	393	424	442	429	466
1981	402	391	424	443	427	466
1982	403	396	426	440	431	467

Table 4

English and American History Scores:
Charlotte-Mecklenburg Schools

Achievement Tests

Year	ENGLISH COMPOSITION			MATH LEVEL I			AMERICAN HISTORY			MATH LEVEL II		
	CMS	NC	National	CMS	NC	National	CMS	NC	National	CMS	NC	National
1974	554		517	563		545	556		531			
1975	563		515	572		545	563		531			
1976	540		532	520		546	533		538			
1977	560	550	516	552	548	547	553	541	533			
1978	575	553	512	569	549	541	579	549	531			
1979	571	557	514	543	548	537	571	553	529			
1980	569	560	518	540	549	536				654	658	653
1981	558	546	512	548	546	539	550	540	508	637	632	654
1982	541	556	520	543	549	545	499	527	511	663	658	661

Table 5

GRADE EQUIVALENT COMPARISONS
C-M Black & White Students
1978-81

CODE:

B = Black
W = White

TOTAL READING

GRADE	1978 B	1978 W	1979 B	1979 W	1980 B	1980 W	1981 B	1981 W
3	2.5	4.0	2.8	4.1	3.1	4.3	3.3	4.4
6	4.6	7.7	5.1	7.9	5.4	8.1	5.7	8.3
9	6.8	10.8	7.0	11.0	7.7	11.2	7.9	11.6

TOTAL MATH

GRADE	1978 B	1978 W	1979 B	1979 W	1980 B	1980 W	1981 B	1981 W
3	3.2	4.0	3.4	4.3	3.5	4.4	3.7	4.5
6	5.4	7.5	5.7	7.6	6.2	8.0	6.5	8.0
9	7.6	10.1	8.0	11.1	8.3	11.9	8.7	12.5

TOTAL LANGUAGE

GRADE	1978 B	1978 W	1979 B	1979 W	1980 B	1980 W	1981 B	1981 W
3	2.6	4.1	3.2	4.6	3.5	4.9	3.7	5.1
6	4.4	8.2	4.8	8.7	5.4	9.6	6.2	10.0
9	6.3	10.9	6.7	11.4	7.7	12.3	8.1	12.9

TOTAL BATTERY

GRADE	1978 B	1978 W	1979 B	1979 W	1980 B	1980 W	1981 B	1981 W
3	2.8	3.9	3.2	4.2	3.4	4.4	3.5	4.5
6	4.9	7.6	5.4	7.8	5.7	8.0	6.2	8.3
9	7.1	10.6	7.5	11.0	8.0	11.4	8.2	12.1

Table 6

Public School Enrollment Trends

In Areas Adjacent to Mecklenburg County

	1971	1982
Geston County	32,000	32,760
Union County	9,954	12,385
Monroe City	3,053	3,227
Lincoln County (North of Charlotte; Untouched by busing)	5,249	8,788
Iredell	10,135	10,065
Lancaster	11,750	11,515
York	20,875	23,010

tional merit of desegregation.

Table 4 reveals that a pattern of either stable or declining performance, similar to that observed on the *SAT*, also occurred on other achievement measures. From 1974 to 1982, English Composition scores declined from 554 to 541. In Math Level I a decline of 563 to 543 is recorded, and a short-term increase (1980-82) is noted in Math Level II, but this is difficult to interpret since pre-desegregation scores are unavailable. The American History drop is 556 to 449.

The litmus test of the desegregation-higher achievement thesis, however, is whether minority students have, in desegregated schools of C-MC, gained higher academic competencies. In *Swann*, McMillan referred to the 1968-69 C-MC racial achievement differential and concluded "...This alarming contrast in performance (black-white achievement gap) is obviously not known to school patrons generally....It is painfully apparent that quality education cannot live in a segregated school: segregation is the greatest barrier to quality education...."(11)

Table 5 summarizes recent achievement test scores. Here, when pre-*Swann* (1968-69) and post-*Swann* test scores of black children are appraised, educational gains have indeed occurred. Thus in 1981, 6th grade blacks and whites scored higher than their 1968-69 counterparts. The differences are rather remarkable. In 1968-69, and in math, the average black and white 6th graders performed at slightly below 4th and mid-5th grade levels, respectively. In 1981 (Table 2), the district-wide 6th grade math average was 7.8. Table 5 breaks down the Table 2 data by race, and shows that in 1981 the average black 6th grade math performance was at mid-6th grade level whereas the white level was at 8th grade. During the period 1978-1981, blacks and whites made striking achievement gains. Compared to 1978 progress levels, 6th grade blacks, over the three year period, registered an average *incremental* gain of 1.8 grade levels in Total Language and over a full year in Total Battery. Incremental gains of this magnitude are clearly at variance with national trends. Something has happened in C-MC.

And yet the size of the 6th grade racial gap in 1981, in grade level units, is about the same as that reported in 1968-69. For example, in math the 1968-69 gap — a score obtained by averaging math differences in the five paired (black and white)

(11)   *Swann*, op. cit., pp. 1296-1297, 1969, as cited in *Hearings*, op. cit., p. 534.

schools cited — was 1.6 (again, in grade-equivalence units). For the years 1978-81, the math gap was 2.1; 1.9; 1.8; and 1.5. Direct content comparisons (recognizing dissimilar times and tests) may also be conducted in the Language area. Here the average 1968-69 gap was 3.3 grade levels; the annual gaps (1978-81) cited in Table 5 are 3.8; 3.9; 4.2; and 3.8.

Table 5 also reveals that the average achievement gaps for 9th graders in 1981 were 3.7 (Reading); 3.8 (Math); 4.8 (Total Language); and 3.9 (Total Battery). In general, this is as wide, or wider, a racial achievement gap as reported in the extensive survey conducted by Coleman in 1966,(12) as well as the 1968-69 gap cited by McMillan in *Swann*. What *has* changed is the elevation of certain scores. Particularly noteworthy is the trend for white norms, at all levels, to be unusually high. Normally it is expected that a group of 3rd, 6th, and 9th grade students will obtain scores around the 3rd, 6th, and 9th grade levels, respectively. Referring again to 1968-69 achievement scores, it is noted that, during the pre-desegregation epoch, whites scored at or above the 6th grade level, or about where national statistics would suggest such students would perform. Contrastingly, in 1981 average white 6th grade scores are significantly higher; the average white score is 8.65 (subtest average: Table 5). Similarly, 9th grade whites are performing as if they are capable of succeeding in senior high school (Table 5). These high scores occur despite evidence, presented later in this paper, that a significant number of middle class students left the C-MC schools. Normally, middle class students perform higher than non-middle class students, but here (Table 5) we have C-MC 3rd, 6th, and 9th graders, deprived of substantial numbers of their middle class counterparts, scoring at unusually high achievement levels.

The reportedly high scores of C-MC whites (and blacks, if we consider national norms) may be associated with various test anomalies such as a low "ceiling effect." For example, when norms of a test are generous, or when other conditions such as "test-teaching" prevail, students may register unusually high scores which are unrepresentative of what the students actually can accomplish under normal testing circumstances, wherein it is rare for students to score at the "ceiling."

If an unusually large number of students score at or near the

(12)   Coleman, James S., et al., *Equality of Educational Opportunity*, Washington, D.C.: U.S. Government Printing Office, 1966.

top limits of the test, then scores are distorted because of the low "test ceiling." Certainly it is unusual for a group of presumably average (to below average, judging from middle class flight in C-MC) 9th grade students to attain (an average of) 12th grade scores. Such inflated white scores can be expected to work in tandem with elevated black scores, but scores of the latter will probably not be so greatly influenced by the "ceiling effect" since fewer numbers of blacks (for whatever reasons) under current conditions will reach the "ceiling." Thus the racial achievement gap may close, under conditions existing in C-MC, if for no reason other than more whites are crowding the ceiling. It therefore seems inappropriate to report elevated scores as evidence that student learning has increased and that desegregation has raised achievement levels.

B. Middle Class Flight

Mobility trends within a school district must be seen within the context of national geographic trends, and C-MC is situated in an area of population growth. This may reflect the nation's concern about energy costs and subsequent southward population drift. C-MC has steadily gained population: the county population was 272,711 in 1960, 354,656 in 1970. With the advent of busing, the C-MC system increased at a rate of approximately 2,500 students per year.

As the decade ended, continued enrollment growth was projected: by the 1974-75 term demographic experts predicted that C-MC schools (grades 1-12) would serve 91,000 students. The actual 1974-75 population was 77,805. Moreover, it was in that year that kindergarten was phased in, so the enrollment included at least 1,000 kindergartners, not included in the early enrollment projections. Therefore, the projected 91,000 would be at least 92,000.

After 1969-70, and related to anticipated mandated busing, the school population in counties adjacent to Mecklenberg increased, as shown in Table 6. There is probably a causal relationship between busing in C-MC and the increase or stability in school populations of schools of counties surrounding C-MC which had little, if any, busing. At the outset of the 1970s, and indeed as of 1981, as noted by Judge McMillan, "...there are hundreds maybe thousands of school districts in North Caro-

Table 7

Statistics On Enrollment

Characteristics and Major Reassignment Plans

In Charlotte-Mecklenburg County

Year	P.S. En-rollment	Non-Public School En-rollment	% Black	Kindergarten Public School Enrollment	Notations
July 1960 Schools Consoli-dated	60,075	2450			
1966-67	76,889	2900	28%		
1967-68	79,696	2950	28%		
1968-69	82,000 (est.)	3000	28%		
1969-70	84,518	2900	29%	830	1) Approximately 900 Title I Kinder-garteners 2) At this point C-MC officials believe that enrollment in public schools adja-cent to C-MC in-creased; concurrent-ly, immigration and births, to and in C-MC, decreased.
1970-71	82,507	5800	30%	985	1) First year of large-scale desegre-gation
1971-72	81,042	6500	31%	801	1) Court approves changes to feeder plan, rather than 3-level plan
1972-73	79,873	6900	32%	837	
1973-74	78,626	7300	33%	1662	1) Minor plan revi-sions

Table 7 (Cont'd)

Year	P.S. En-rollment	Non-Public School En-rollment	% Black	Kindergarten Public School Enrollment	Notations
1974-75	77,805	7700	34%	2429	1) An estimated 10,000 students af-fected by major plan revision 2) Kindergarten phased in
1975-76	78,257	8000	35%	3114	
1976-77	80,507	8050	36%	5744	1) Kindergarten a-vailable throughout district 2) School officials report a greater loss of pupils (502) than anticipated.
1977-78	79,465	8250	36%	5268	
1978-79	77,609	8400	37%	4888	1) Revised plan changes attendence regulations for 4,850 students
1979-80	76,305	8650	37%	4705	
1980-81	74,149	8850 including an estimated 750 blacks--- there are few non-public kindergartens	38%	4745	1) 48,966 students are transported, including 21,210 blacks
1981-82	72,905		38%	4710	1) Revised assign-ments given 1,020 students
1982-83	71,890 + 272 in Metro-Cen-ter, total 72,162		39%	5015	

lina, and most of them aren't under court order to desegregate."(13) Further study may reveal that the student enrollment stability and/or increases in districts adjacent to C-MC may be explained by the absence of busing.

Stability of the peer group is a significant component to quality education, and it was assumed that further student reassignments would be unnecessary, after the initial *Swann* order. In affirming *Swann* the high court ruled that once a district is desegregated, and barring evidence of deliberate segregatory activity, the system would be unitary. The Court declared that "It does not follow that the communities served by school systems will remain demographically stable, for in a growing, mobile society, few will do so. Neither school authorities nor district courts are constitutionally required to make year-by-year adjustments of the racial composition of student bodies once the affirmative duty to desegregate has been accomplished..."

McMillan's ruling stipulated that no school operate with an all black or predominantly black student body. But it also emphasized that the goal was diversity, not racial balance. A wide range of inter-school racial percentages was permitted, extending from 3% black at Bain Elementary to 41% at Cornelius. This latter stipulation again was consistent with the high court's determination that "...the constitutional command to desegregate schools does not mean that every school in every community must always reflect the racial composition of the school system as a whole. It should be clear that the existence of some small number of one-race, or virtually one-race, schools within a district is not in and of itself the mark of a system which still practices segregation by law...."(14)

Since 1969, the C-MC schools have required far more frequent reassignments than was anticipated. In the fall of 1981, C-MC superintendent Jay M. Robinson stated that the original assignment plan was modified in 1974, 1978, 1979, and 1981. Actual school records indicate that there have been at least five, and not four, reassignment plans. Table 7 reveals that, following the 1970-71 academic year, which witnessed the first year of large-scale busing, court-approved changes in 1971-72 permitted reassignments based on a new feeder plan. Changes in the feeder plan were approved by the Court in 1971-72. Minor

(13) *Hearings,* op. cit., p. 523.
(14) *Swann,* op. cit.

plan revisions were carried out in 1973-74; in 1974-75, about 10,000 students were affected by a major reassignment plan. In 1977, HEW expressed dissatisfaction with racial balance. (15) New assignment changes affected 4,850 students in 1978-79; three years later an additional 1,020 students were reassigned for purposes of racial balance.

Almost a decade after *Swann,* in 1978, a reporter from *U.S. News and World Report* observed "...Almost every year (C-MC) students have had to be shifted to different schools to maintain the prescribed 70% white, 30% black ratio...So much white loss has occurred that the 70-30 requirement is now abandoned. The new goal is to prevent any school enrollment from being more than half black. Some children spend more than an hour traveling distances up to 21 miles to school...."(16)

More than a decade after *Swann,* Superintendent Robinson informed a congressional subcommittee that each C-MC scool ranges from 20 to 50% black with the exception of one elementary school which has a 90% black enrollment. (17) In the same hearings, McMillan informed congressional leaders that "...ratios of the schools have varied all over the lot. The first order I entered was 3 to 41% (black) and the ratios today — if I recall the facts correctly — are somewhere between 17 and 85% or so. There are 8 or 10 that are more than half black in a community that is about one-third black...The ratio has never been anything magic or inviolate...."(18) But official C-MC enrollment figures challenge the Robinson-McMillan claims. In September 1982, 42 of 75 elementary schools were at or in excess of 41% black, as were 9 of 22 junior high and 6 of 11 senior high schools; 10 schools had more than 50% and 2 had exactly 50%. The ratios varied from 19 to 95% black.

McMillan also informed congressional leaders that after 1975 there has been no significant increase in private schools, no great change in black/white ratios. Private schools, of course, cost money and in a depressed economy many parents are priced out of the market. They can't afford to resettle or trans-

(15)   Clements, W. Lamar, Chief, Elementary and Secondary Education Branch Office for Civil Rights, Department of Health, Education and Welfare, Atlanta, April 8, 1977: Letter to Dr. John Phillips, Acting Superintendent of C-MC Schools, April 8, 1977.
(16)   *U.S. News and World Report,* May 8, 1978.
(17)   *Hearings,* op. cit.
(18)   *Hearings,* op. cit.

fer their children to private schools, but such parents are likely to be traumatically unhappy with the (public) schools their children attend: that unhappiness can create ripple effects throughout families, schools, and communities. Before the middle class flight question is sorted out it would be useful to administer a questionnaire to parents. This questionnaire could ascertain how many (black and white) parents would send their children to a private school if they could afford it. And yet, despite recessionary economic conditions, and as shown on Table 7, private school school enrollment increased from 8,000 to 8,850 from 1975-76 to the spring of 1981, while public school enrollment declined from 78,257 to 74,149. Moreover, public school kindergarten enrollment since 1975 rose from 3,114 to 5,015 in 1982. Therefore, if the kindergarten factor is equalized, the public school loss during this period is substantial although incalculatable, because complete figures are curiously unavailable.

Table 7 also shows that private school enrollment, in 1969-70, constituted 3.43% of the public school enrollment. By 1981-82, and excluding kindergarten students, it had risen to 13%. This suggests that the C-MC schools may have lost a large proportion of social class parents: expert testimony in *Milliken* estimated that between 10 and 20% of Detroit-area pupils were from high social-class homes. (19) If these figures are representative of C-MC, then large numbers of parents — as many as two-thirds — of the high social class population no longer enroll their children in C-MC, a figure not unrealistic in view of enrollment trends observed in public school districts adjacent to C-MC (Table 6).

Conclusion

This paper has appraised the impact of mandated desegregation in the C-MC public schools, with respect to 1) academic performance of blacks and 2) student stability as this is measured through middle class flight. Advocates of desegregation have historically asserted that desegregation would enhance black learning and not seriously disrupt student stability, it being generally recognized that students derive social-emotional strengths from proceeding through school with essentially the same peer groups.

(19) Wolf, Eleanor P. *Trial and Error: The Detroit School Segregation Case,* Detroit: Wayne State University Press, 1981, p. 223.

Longitudinal data from C-MC question both pro-busing assumptions. It appears that desegregation has not enabled black students, as a group, to acquire greater academic competencies; moreover, it is difficult to arrive at any conclusion other than that C-MC desegregation has disrupted student stability profiles by accelerating the flight of black and white middle class students from the public schools. These findings are particularly discouraging, since the data were drawn from a school district wherein all student cohorts entered kindergarten in a school district which had been racially desegregated. There fore, the observed racial achievement gap cannot be ascribed to segregated schools. The findings reported here, if replicated, suggest that serious reconsideration should be given to the use of mandated desegregation as a remedy which presumably enhances life prospects for many of the nation's most vulnerable youth.

"PUSH-THROUGH" EDUCATIONAL PROGRAMS:
THREAT TO ACADEMIC INTEGRITY
AND TO THE NATION'S ECONOMIC PRODUCTIVITY

In this final paper the author shows how the current drive for ethnic "equality" is distorting the U.S. educational process, resulting in the falsification of the entire system by "push-through" programs.

It is generally recognized that quality education is essential to industrial productivity in today's complex economies. (1) Well-educated workers are presumably more skilled and productive in dealing with the growing demands of technological industries and businesses. Current circumstances suggest that the productivity-educational linkage is not coincidental: the United States currently experiences a virtually unbroken series of deficit trade balances at a time of increasing evidence that American students fare poorly on achievement tests in international comparisons with their foreign counterparts. (2)

Within recent years a number of foreign leaders have attributed a perceived decline of American influence in world affairs to schooling-productivity issues which are linked to the pluralistic nature of American society. When discussing American trade deficits, and in an off-guard remark, Japanese Prime Minister Yasuhiro Nakasone stated that "the U.S. intellectual level is lower than that of Japan because of the presence of blacks,* Puerto Ricans and Mexicans." (3) Seeking to clarify Nakasone's remarks, Japanese party spokesmen said that he meant literacy level and not intellectual level. This distinction, attributing Japanese-U.S. productivity differentials to questions of learning rather than of intellectual potential, was more palatable to Americans but places an obvious burden on American schools to raise the educational productivity of minorities. Shortly after Nakasone's statement, and again in the context of industrial productivity, Soviet leader Mikhail Gorbachev suggested that the United States solve its racial problems by setting up separate states for blacks and other minorities. (4)

Remarks by Nakasone and Gorbachev indicate that foreign

---

* This paper deals primarily with educational issues involving America's largest minority, blacks. It is recognized however that there are many American minorities, for each minority, government sanctioned compensatory measures may have different effects. Statistical evidence of ethnic group differences are cited but it is clear that issues of superiority/inferiority are not involved since vast inter-group and intra-group distinctions exist. In general, for example, on achievement and IQ scores approximately 15% of blacks equal or exceed the white average; the scores of approximately 84% of whites equal or exceed the black average.

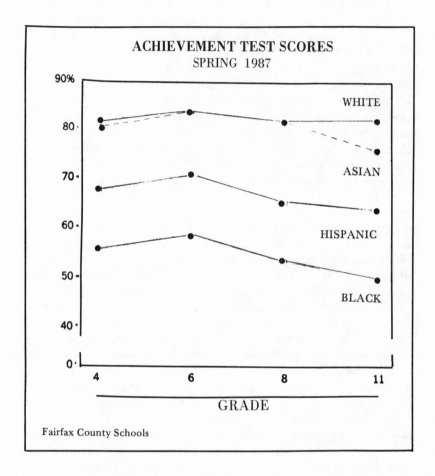

The disparity between SAT scores achieved by students of diverse ethnic groups in the United States is exemplified by this graph published in 1987 by the Fairfax County Public Schools (Northern Virginia). Fairfax County prides itself on its school system and upon its efforts to aid minority children. (*Washington Post*, June 30, 1987)

leaders are monitoring U.S. minority issues, which demographics indicate will become increasingly significant in the future as the U.S. seeks to maintain its role as a world leader. Some of the statistics are grim and suggest the need for reexamining compensatory schooling measures intended to raise minority learning levels. Blacks' dropout rates are now more than double those of whites, and this rate is significantly correlated with employability.(5) In some cities as many as 50% of young black males find themselves under-educated and unemployed; while the national unemployment rate is 6.9%, it is 15% for black males.(6) In every metropolitan area a black subculture has become entrenched, and the job situation for young blacks has become steadily worse since the initiation of preferential programs. In 1950 the unemployment rate for young blacks was 1.5 times greater than for young whites; now it is more than twice as great.(7) These figures are indeed ominous if educational competencies are associated with productivity. Between 1970-1985, blacks, Hispanics and other minorities supplied 18.4% of the work force addition. This figure may be compared with an estimated 29% between 1985 and 2000.(8)

Forced Busing:* Can American Social Scientists Objectify Racial Issues?

Despite evidence that minorities experience high rates of educational vulnerability, that eduction is central to effective productivity, and that minorities will comprise a greater proportion of the nation's future work force, few if any Americans seriously anticipate that the United States will modify its position on race relations as some foreigners might propose. But both at home and abroad there is a growing sense that those who set American schooling policies have not only been reluctant to deal straightforwardly with sensitive questions but that social scientists have seriously erred in appraising the consequences of compensatory measures which are interlaced with racial matters. Consider the policy of "forced busing," which has required millions of school children to be daily bused out of their own residential areas in order that American

---

* As used here, forced busing is considered synonymous with most school desegregation undertakings which are race-conscious efforts to balance the public schools by race, thus prohibiting some children from attending their neighborhood school attendance centers.

classrooms might comprise designated ratios of black and white students.

For over three decades numbers of American educators have proclaimed the merits of forced busing. This expensive and disruptive practice was initially justified by the assumption that black students would learn more effectively if they sat in classrooms which contained a number of whites. Despite annual costs that ran into billions of dollars the American (busing = black achievement) thesis went virtually unchallenged until the mid-1980s.(9) The National Institute of Education (NIE) then undertook a comprehensive study, designed to determine whether busing did enable blacks to learn more effectively. The nation's leading scholastic proponents of desegregation were unable to identify a single study which demonstrated that busing improved the long-term achievement profiles of blacks.(10) Nonetheless, and apparently because busing is a sensitive issue, those who shape national schooling policies continue to report desegregatory achievement benefits,(11) and even proclaim that blacks who participate in busing programs as schoolchildren are more likely as adults to obtain better jobs.(12) Careful attention to actual statistics demonstrates that neither claim can be empirically supported.(13)

It certainly could be argued that if the nation's leading spokesmen for busing cannot concede what the statistics clearly indicate, then genuine schooling reform is unattainable and the United States will continue to divert enormous resources into futile and educationally unproductive programs. Fortunately, recent developments suggest that viable reform is feasible. This hope springs from evidence that blacks are demanding educational accountability, now more than ever before. Mainstream blacks no longer uncritically support the position of civil rights leaders, whose careers have been built upon an insistence on the perpetuation of these race-conscious but unproductive programs.(14) Simply put, minority issues can no longer be simplistically moralized through racial polarization.

Are "Push-Through" Programs Discouraging Minorities from Developing their Potentials?

Schooling provides one of the main vehicles for later employability, and in this paper I contend that American educators have been literally coerced into implementing "push-through" programs for minorities, all the way from kindergarten through college. Such programs encourage school personnel to think of students not as individuals but as members of a group. Emphasis, therefore, is not placed on the development of individualized learning programs so that individuals, whether black or white, may later as adults draw upon marketable skills. Instead, the educators' attention is riveted on the establishment and maintenance of ethnic quotas in every component of the learning process. To meet the required quotas, students are uncritically passed from grade to grade. The final stage of the educational process ends with matriculation, when inordinately high numbers of blacks receive high school or college degrees without having acquired the requisite skills commensurate with those degrees. The burden then shifts to employers who, to avoid economic penalties and possible legal proceedings, are obligated to use race-conscious employment practices, and carry members of designated ethnic groups at various levels on their payrolls, whether or not these individuals are able to pull their weight. Small wonder that U.S. businesses are not fully competitive in the world market.

This system punishes virtually all groups within American society: the more qualified blacks whose authentic competencies are less likely to be recognized because of the stigma that blacks must receive special treatment; the less qualified blacks who are denied appropriate opportunities to develop skills that are later marketable and who often realize that they owe their degree and/or their job to patronage. Whites are also penalized, and become embittered when they conclude that it doesn't pay for white males to acquire skills, since they'll be passed over in the job market because of reverse discrimination. At all levels the schooling processes are mediocretized, and the nation's productivity is reduced while foreign competitors are handed a competitive edge.

Illustrations of "push-through" policies in favor of inadquate performance can be drawn from virtually every feature of elementary and secondary school programs. Suspensions, disciplinary actions, grades and special class placements are based in the U.S. today not on educational considerations but on race.(15) For this there is good reason. Monitoring committees at the Federal, state, and local levels periodically examine the progress of blacks and whites. These committees rarely assess policy implications from statistics which reveal that blacks at every grade level score lower on achievement tests than do whites and therefore it is likely that their grades will be lower. Similarly, monitoring committees characteristically overlook social class factors which partially explain the high black incidence of behavioral disorders, delinquency and crime. Many disadvantaged blacks are among the big losers of this benign tolerance. For them, schools often represent the last available organized institutional support system, before their lives stabilize into patterns of employability or unemployability.

At every grade level there are vast differences in students' learning needs, and historically teachers have been encouraged to deal with individual differences, but in the United States educationally relevant individual distinctions are often denied. IQ tests, for example, have long served as useful measures in setting academic strategies. While aptitude tests have their limitations, they have provided teachers with useful insights concerning objectives to be pursued, and most experts in testing and curriculum support the use of IQ measures since if some people are brighter than others the curriculum should adapt to what individual students can achieve.(16) Of course it is assumed that the limitations of the IQ metric be recognized and that each child receive maximum classroom challenge.(17) But because of persistant racial differences in performance in IQ tests, some reformers have opted for the elimination of IQ tests altogether. Says one critic, often an expert witness in civil rights litigation: "IQ scores represent the contemporaneous justification for maintaining the inferiority of minorities and children from low-income famies."(18)

Always controversial, the concept of IQ became an incendiary issue after school districts abolished school segregation, and placed black and white children in the same instructional groups. Students' IQs had traditionally served as useful instructional guides in assignments to different ability groups — usually high, middle and low. Circumstances changed with forced busing. Social class controls often collapsed as housing patterns no longer determined where chilren attended school. Large numbers of lower social class blacks and whites began attending school with middle class whites and blacks. Under these changed conditions and when IQ was used as a criterion for grouping, most advanced classes contained a disproportionate number of whites; large numbers of blacks were assigned to classes which dealt with less challenging curricula. Unequal ethnic ratios were particularly noticeable at both ends of the IQ spectrum: few blacks were in classes for the gifted; few whites were placed in classes for the mentally retarded.(19)

Charging that IQ tests were biased and resulted in excessive numbers of blacks identified as mentally retarded, in the early 1970s a group of black U.S. psychologists filed a class action suit, *Larry P. vs. Riles*.(20) After more than a decade of litigation, school districts in seven Western states were forbidden from using IQ tests to evaluate black students for placement in special educational classes. In this ruling the judges stepped to a different drummer than most experts in intelligence testing. One extensive study, involving an anonymous questionnaire, reported that testing experts overwhelmingly supported the use of IQ tests. On an even more controversial note the experts endorsed the view that heredity significantly affects IQ; a majority of the respondents reported that they considered IQ differences between races and social classes to be somewhat hereditary.(21)

With the outlawing of IQ testing, school administrators turned to unlikely substitutes. In 1984, San Francisco school psychologists were prohibited from using IQ tests and were asked to "be creative" in determining students' eligibility for special education classes until new methods arrived.(22) For a year, the psychologists mostly marked time and applied guesswork in determining which students qualified for special programs. After about a year, the replacement test was announced: *Feuerstein's Learning Potential Assessment Device (LPAD)*. For those who assume that environment essentially shapes human development, the *LPAD* was the perfect instrument. In 15 years of experimental work in Israel, Feuerstein has essentially ignored children's IQs and assumed that the intellectual performance of all children can be "transmuted into higher and more dynamic functions."(23) Not only is there no evidence that the *LPAD* has validly identified various types of learning problems; the *LPAD* manual specifically and repeatedly cautions that the test should not be used to categorize, classify or determine eligibility for special education.(24) Unrestrained by a test that lacks validity and reliability, school personnel are now free to use race quotas as a factor in deciding which children qualify for various special classes. There should be fewer complaints that too many blacks are placed in rooms for the mentally retarded and too many whites in classes for the gifted.

Some schools districts have employed procedures other than the *LPAD* to deal with the IQ test ban. In *Larry P. vs. Riles*, the courts concluded that IQ tests contained cultural bias and that greater consideration should be given to students' social and cultural backgrounds in assessing intellectual capabilities. Some testing authorities interpreted this as an invitation to equalize the IQs of blacks, whites and Hispanics. Consequently Jane Mercer, a key plaintiff witness in *Larry P*, developed the *System of Multicultural Pluralistic Assessment (SOMPA)* which reportedly "heralds the beginning of nondiscrimination assessment."(25)

The *SOMPA* awards bonus IQ points to students with "disadvantaged" backgrounds. Its use is more ludicrous than a physician adjusting the scales to allow an obese patient handicap points to run a marathon. The *SOMPA* manual and college textbooks illustrate how the *SOMPA* permits psychologists to instantly raise the IQs of black students. Example: a black child's Full Scale IQ increases 21 points after special credits are given because he is black, comes from a broken family and has parents who failed to obtain a high school education. With consideration for his background, the child no longer has a borderline intelligence: his "new" IQ is above average and teachers are encouraged to provide more challenging classwork.(26) Many experienced teachers recognize this as a prescription for failure. Assigned work he cannot do, the child is likely to become frustrated and discouraged and to disengage from learning. These circumstances have become so common in racially desegregated schools that researchers have coined a term to describe the behaviors which frequently characterize black students upon whom unrealistic educational expectations are placed: "alienation," a syndrome "consisting of feelings of pessimism, cynicism, distrust, apathy and emotional distance."(27) The *SOMPA* and other "cultural fair" tests have created additional burdens for school personnel. After all, if there are no ethnic IQ differences, then schools, and school personnel, are responsible for any significant gap in black-white learning levels, or for racial imbalance in classrooms or ability groups.

After devising strategies to reduce or eliminate the black-white IQ gap, educational reformers focused on achievement test differentials. Research had invariably revealed that, as a group, whites surpassed blacks on achievement measures from kindergarten through college.(29) Therefore more whites received advanced assignments, and a higher proportion of them obtained diplomas and degrees. This troubled some civil rights advocates. Exercising creativity, they developed strategies to increase prospects that blacks and whites receive similar schooling experiences, irrespective of the skills individual students possessed. Two strategies were assigned highest priority: insisting that schools substitute ability or homogeneous groupings with heterogeneous grouping, and using tests which yield inflated scores, thereby masking the true extent of black educational disadvantage.

Very early in the civil rights movement, the NAACP and others interpreted ability grouping in racially imbalanced school as evidence of "within-school segregation."(29) In virtually every desegregated school district, whites were more heavily concentrated in advanced classes whereas blacks were more concentrated in less advanced classes. Pressure mounted for heterogeneous grouping or assignment of students to instructional groups regardless of ability. This strategy permits techniques such as "team learning," where more advanced students help the less advanced. There is no evidence that black children benefit from "teaming" and, in practice, more blacks than whites end up requiring help or being the subservient members of the "team." This fosters alienation with all the attendant signs of shame, incompetence, and anger. Such a situation does not help those black students whose abilities qualify them for membership of more advanced classes.(30) Such superior black students suffer as much as superior white students.

Heterogeneous grouping produces other problems. Teachers report that it is considerably more difficult to teach a classroom consisting of students with widely varying academic skills.(31) School desegregation has exacerbated teachers' difficulties in providing for students' individualized learning needs since the range of abilities within classrooms broadens when classrooms are made up of large numbers of black and of white students.(32) For example, in a typical heterogeneous tenth grade racially desegregated classroom, the skill level ranges from third grade through the second year of college. Most high school teachers have from 25 to 35 students in from four to six classes a day.

With 100 to 200 students daily, many teachers assign lessons designed for the average ability level. Consequently those students — black or white — who read at the third grade level are frustrated; students capable of reading at the college level are bored. Only the overbearing political goals of heterogeneous grouping remains: instructional groupings of students are racially balanced.

Under the prevailing U.S. legal and political climate, school administrators resort to other strategems in order to deal with political pressures associated with ethnic educational differences. One of the more popular of these is use of achievement tests which produce misleadingly high scores and distort the true magnitude of the ethnic achievement gap. With ethnic differences artificially reduced through statistical games, the required heterogeneous grouping appears to be more appropriate, and inflated test scores suggest the reasonableness of passing marginal students from grade to grade.

In recent years the *California Achievement Test (CAT)* has grown in popularity. On this measure it is not unusual for most of the white and some of the black students to obtain *maximum* scores.(33) Consequently better students are denied an opportunity to demonstrate just *how* competent they are. With the upper range of test scores capped, less competent students fare considerably better in comparison with students who have topped the test. This permits school administrators to report that poor and disadvantaged students have narrowed the achievement gap; because of general social class conditions this results in an apparent improvement in black students' academic attainments. In fact, it is impossible to estimate the true ethnic achievement differences unless test results fairly provide for all students to fully demonstrate their abilities in all achievement areas.

As students near completion of high school, the significance of racial differences acquires a new dimension. In many school districts and throughout the elementary and secondary years, variables are manipulated to equalize the IQs, achievement levels, suspension rates, grades, and special class placements of blacks and whites. But as graduation nears, some districts employ minimum competency testing (MCT) to determine who should get a diploma, which presumably represents a specified skill level in such achievement spheres as reading and mathematics. The high school diploma is often a requisite to higher education or to accessing certain jobs.

Early efforts to impose minimum competency testing (MCT) as a graduate requirement were thwarted: civil rights groups insisted that the high black failure rate was associated with segregated schooling which busing would correct. That argument now lacks viability since all American schools have been desegregated for more than a dozen years.(34) Where MCT occurs, blacks as a class continue to suffer a higher incidence of academic failure than whites. Moreover, tutoring blacks for MCT has been generally ineffective, even after second and third test administrations.(35) Presently there is no evidence that a single school district has denied diplomas on the basis of low academic attainments; in every major city of the United States diplomas are given to students with third to fifth grade grade reading and math skills. Nationally the average black high school graduate reads about 3.5 grade levels below the average white graduate. For black women the ethnic gap is somewhat smaller, for black males somewhat larger.(36)

Preferential Admissions for Minorities and Charges of College Racism

Largely ignoring students' academic deficiencies, institutions of higher education perpetuate the "pass-through" policies of public schools and admit marginal students, a disproportionate number of them black. Some researchers consider preferential admissions a primary reason for rising racial tensions on American campuses.(37) Blacks frequently feel uncomfortable on largely white campuses and 80% of them report that they have sensed some form of racial discrimination.(38) The problem of campus unrest is not localized and the troubled universities include some of the nation's most prestigious: Purdue, UCLA, University of Massachusetts, the University of Michigan, Amherst.(39) The recent increase in racial violence has surprised and puzzled university administrators who are uncertain how to respond. But Glen Loury, a black Harvard professor, theorizes that "push-through" policies of the elementary and secondary schools help produce the persisting black achievement gap which, coupled with a widely recognized policy of preferential college admissions — favoring less competent minority students at the expense of more competent white students who are deprived admission — may be a chief cause of racial strife.(40)

An examination of black complaints supports Loury's hypothesis. "It's not blatant," says one of the black students. Discrimination does not appear to be deliberate; rather it spreads from a pervasive perception of competency. "It's like you're the last person picked as a lab partner, or someone will lean over you and ask the person next to you. what the professor said — like you wouldn't have understood it."(41) Other blacks complain that white students will study and share notes, but not involve them. These complaints suggest that the origins of much campus unrest may not lie in race but in the perceived academic competency of the students themselves, or in other words, in a system of preferential admissions which invites racial stigma. Certainly it is difficult to fault students, who want to succeed academically, if they gravitate toward those whom they view as the more competent among their peers.

Some blacks also allege racist faculty attitudes. A typical charge is that professors have low expectations of minorities, minorities, notice absences and late submissions, and have a general feeling that minorities will make the bottom of the class.(42) Since the average black high school graduate, and college student, reads more than three grade levels below the white average,(43) professors' perceptions may, unfortunately, rest on experience. If in fact, professors expect all black students to read at the level expected of all whites, it is difficult to envision any scenario other than one which invites alienation.

Much of the racial difficulty experienced in higher education appears related to preferential policies which were hastily devised with little appraisal of consequences for those blacks who were unready or unable to succeed in standard college work. From 1950 to 1976, policies of preferential admission for minorities received high priority at most colleges. During that period the percentage of blacks in four year institutions more than tripled, peaking at 10.3% in the mid-1970s, but then declining.(44) Activists ascribe the recent slight decline in the proportion of blacks in colleges to racism; they prefer to ignore the ongoing crisis in the ghetto which has contributed to the steady post-1970 rise in dropout rates and has left increasing numbers of blacks less equipped for college success.

In higher education, "push-through" advocates encounter a

familiar adversary, the IQ test, somewhat modified in the form of measures such as the *Scholastic Aptitude Test (SAT)* which most institutions employ as one of several screening techniques to shape admission policies. Nationally, black students' scores on tests such as the *SAT* indicate that should college admission require performance at the national average, or fiftieth percentile, the number of black students on campuses would be significantly reduced. In 1985, for example, 26% of black high school graduates enrolled in college. Surprisingly, and apparently because of general ghetto conditions which are sometimes unrelated to intellectual ability, there are no significant ability differences between black dropouts and high school graduates.(45) Therefore, and in view of national learning profiles, if colleges admitted *all* blacks with *SAT* scores equal to the national average, then 16% rather than 26% of black high school graduates would go on to higher education.(46) These figures suggest that large numbers of black students with *SAT* scores significantly below average manage to enroll in college and that the instrument is far from being consistently used as a screening device if colleges are to maintain standard educational requirements.

While many university administrators apparently ignore *SAT* results, there is a sound basis for employing these as one criterion. Studies have shown that *SAT* scores correlate with achievement measures, such as reading and math, which are critical to college success, and also that the instrument identifies students who are likely to fail if granted college admission.(47)

Despite the instrument's validity and reliability, the *SAT* is under attack. Recently the NCAA proposed that all college athletic recuits should have a grade point average of 2.0 (equal to C) and a minimum combined *SAT* score of 700. Critics responded by charging the NCAA with racism, since 55% of black college students have scores of 700 or less, compared to only 14% of white.(48) Conversely there are those who joust with the NAACP on the NCAA issue: they argue that an *SAT* score of 700 equates to an educably retarded score on the American Association of Mental Deficiencies standards as applied during the pre-desegregation era. They further argue that unless colleges downscale their curricula, few blacks with *SAT*s under 700 will succeed academically.(49) Actually, the black failure rate at largely white colleges is five to eight times that of whites, and a long-term study of University of Minnesota black athletes revealed that fewer than 10% actually graduated.(50) Additionally, two separate studies of blacks admitted under preferential conditions reported failure rates of 37% and 49% after their cohorts attended college for only four semesters.(51)

University administrators, faced by discouraging black dropout and achievement rates, are inclined to ignore the complex reasons why one black student drops out of high school for every two who graduate.(52) Instead, they aggressively seek to increase the number of blacks on campus. In June 1987 a group of liberal arts schools including Pomona, Williams, Amherst, Johns Hopkins, Swarthmore and Occidental, met to devise new ways to enroll more minority group students.(53) Already some of the colleges pursue zealous recruitment tactics by going from door to door, searching for likely students in pool halls and even on street corners, to enlist additional blacks in colleges.(54) More than a few unemployed and astonished young blacks have been lured into college, with no questions asked about their academic skills or reading levels.

This uncritical admission of minorities is partially justified in the minds of the recruiters by the belief that test scores, IQ or achievement, can be discarded, and academic deficiencies remedied. The American Council on Education reports that a number of colleges presently spend as much as 25% of their total budgets on special remedial programs, largely designed to provide minority students with academic success.(55) However, there is no published evidence that even one of these programs has increased prospects for collegiate success. Given the facts that many young minority high school students are encouraged to attend college, expect help to succeed, and experience crushing defeat as a result of their inability to cope with the intellectual demands and psychological rigor of higher education, it is little wonder that many have come to perceive the white college university as "racist, corrupt, morally bankrupt and unresponsive to the oppressed."(56)

Black anger on white compuses is a relatively new phenomenon. While a return to segregated universities in the U.S. is not anticipated, the relatively brief history of black students on formerly white campuses explains a good deal of the tension presently surrounding higher education. Integration on white campuses came quickly and with little comprehensive planning. In 1960, 96% of all blacks enrolled in institutions of higher education were securing their education in historic black colleges

(HBC). By 1973 the proportion had declined to 25%.(57) Until 1967, 80% of all undergraduate degrees awarded black students were earned at traditionally black colleges; in 1979, 56% of those were conferred in predominantly white schools.(58) At white colleges, black students generally encountered higher expectations than those prevailing at HBC; unsurprisingly, blacks report that they had to be more vigilant and were more distrustful at white colleges.(59) Conversely, they are more assertive and self-confident at HBC.(60) Jacqueline Fleming argues that black students enjoy enhanced opportunities for academic survival at HBC, where they make larger learning strides.(61)

To say that blacks are less stressed and learn more in HBC does not require that one should go as far as Mr. Gorbachev's conclusion that the United States should establish separate states on the basis of race. However, black attitudes and learning styles at historic black colleges, coupled with extensive black alienation at white institutions, call into question the value of preferential admission policies which may be more counterproductive than contributory as solutions to the problem of providing appropriate educational opportunities to all individuals in racially diverse mixed societies.

After High School and College:
The Final Cost of Educational Patronage

"Push-through" programs may be described as benign efforts to equip blacks for equitable job opportunities and to create ethnic balance in the professions and work force. Available research suggests that, on the job and as a group, the average black performance falls below that of the average white despite or perhaps because of race-conscious policies to and through the college levels. After appraising the impact of affirmative action, Jencks concluded that it was in the economic interests of employers to discriminate against blacks since, as a group, they were less productive. He therefore urged government action so that employers paid heavily for practices which hire and promote on the basis of objective and work-relevant measures.(62) A careful reading of Feinberg's research indicates that he arrives at essentially the same conclusion.(63)

Apparently frustrated when race-conscious methods fail to enable blacks to be equitably placed on the job market, some social critics have questioned established personnel practices.

Researchers deplore as racist the inclination of personnel officials to assign a high proportion of black male high school graduates to lower paying positions, and to insist on the relevance of applicants' reading and math skills.(64) In the continual emphasis on preferential treatment and racial proportionality beyond college and into the job market, personal competency and productivity are denigated as if they were irrelevant in a world that becomes ever more competitive.

On the job, ethnic differences persist and are particularly apparent in education, which is a preferred professional field for blacks; approximately half of all PhDs awarded to blacks are in education.(65) Rather surprisingly, blacks themselves appear to expect that they will fare poorly on competency testing. When the Texas legislature mandated teacher testing in 1984 in an effort to improve the state's public schools, and before the characteristics of the tests were even defined or agreed upon, blacks and Hispanics protested. They expected that their respective minorities would experience high failure rates.(66) Their prediction was accurate in Texas as well as in other states. When Florida administered teacher competency testing, the pass rate for whites was 80% while that of the blacks ranged between 35% and 40%.(67) Nationally, black failure rates have been so high that one black publication charged that the testing movement threatened to "screen blacks out of the teaching profession."(68) Perhaps the more pressing question concerns the effect on students, black and white, of teachers of whatever race who, benefitting from "education's dirty little secret,"(69) graduated from high school and college and have had conferred on them the awesome task of teaching in the nation's troubled public schools.

Preferential educational policies have contributed to ethnic differences in virtually every sphere of the work force. The pattern is consistent: a high proportion of minorities pass through high school and college without acquiring the requisite skills. The American Petroleum Institute administered the *Diagnostic Reading Tests* to job applicants, and found that black applicants read four grade levels below white applicants. The API concluded that white applicants have reading skills "well matched to the industry's reading materials while the reading skills of black applicants are marginal at best."(70) In New York City, $500,000 was spent by court order to produce a job-relevant and nondiscriminatory test; nonetheless, the pass rate for black police officers was 1.6% compared to 10.6% for whites.(71) The low scores of black applicants to medical school has raised concerns about what can be done to increase the number of black physicians without compromising the quality of medical care.(72) Ironically, recent research strongly suggests that well intentioned and race-sensitive educational policies have contributed to ethnic disparities reported in virtually all job categories, and have thus exacerbated unemployment conditions for America's burgeoning minority underclass.(73)

Toward "Color-Blind" and More Productive Schooling

To an important extent, the future of American economic productivity depends upon educational strategies devised within our schools. Effective learners are more likely to become happy and productive adults. In an ethnically monolithic nation such as Japan, educators focus largely on instructional objectives. This contrasts with U.S. pluralistic schooling policies, which for political reasons are obligated to place emphasis on ethnic considerations.

Since the 1950s, American schools have diverted enormous financial and intellectual resources into efforts designed to promote equity. Authentic ethnic differences have been largely ignored and questionable practices undertaken in an effort to artificially reduce the magnitude of minority and white student IQ and achievement profiles. This has produced two main consequences. First, the real educational needs of students have often been subverted to political objectives. Many teachers have found that it is more important to provide similar experiences to equal numbers of black and white students than to deliver appropriate individualized instruction. Secondly, educational standards have been subverted to legal and political considerations; too often students have been uncritically promoted through the public schools and frequently into college, only to suffer academic failure or to obtain devalued diplomas which have little meaning or utility in the world of work.

Blacks have paid a particularly high price for the political expediency which has marked American schools for the past thee decades. Since the 1950s, black dropout and unemployment rates have steadily moved upward, despite burgeoning and race-conscious compensatory programs. Courtland Milloy remarks that "Never in history have there been so many black

youths about to become adults without an iota of job experience. Ill-prepared, arrogant and with unusually high expectations, they can be expected to create social and political
problems that cause havoc in the neighborhoods first, then
spill over to take a toll on the system"(74)

Minorities will consitute an increasingly large proportion of
our work force in future years. If the United States is to remain
the leader of the free world it must begin the difficult task of
rethinking educational priorities. More attention must be direct-
ed to the vastly divergent needs of individual learners within the
schools and where possible this should be done during the early
years; the race of the student should be deemphasized if not
altogether ignored. After all, ethnicity is an irrelevant variable
in any educational enterprise characterized by productivity and
equity.

FOOTNOTES

(1)   "What is culture's role in economic policy," *Wall Street Journal*, December
22, 1986, p. 1; Ramirez, Maria. *Bulletin: Center for Multinational and Comparative
Education*, State Education Department, State of New York, Albany, April-May,
1987; Cuomo, Mario. Address to graduates of Grinnell College, Grinnell, Iowa, May
18, 1987.

(2)   Separate international studies of elementary and secondary students have
reported that Americans have scored at or near the bottom (Flunking the Test.
America's Future, February 1984, pp. 2-3. In comparison with their counterparts
in seven other industrialized countries, U.S. students ranked last in math and not
much better in science and geography. Also, Grant W. Vance: Organization for
Economic Cooperation on Development. *A Resume of the Survey of the Inter-
national Association for the Evaluation of Education Achievement*. Paris, 1974.
Also, Lantor, Linda. "Iowa high schools slipping behind world in math education."
Des Moines Register, May 17, 1987, p. 1. Lantor reports findings of the Second
International Math Studies which examine learning profiles in twenty countries or
educational systems. American twelfth graders were only ahead of three groupings:
British Columbia (Canada), Thailand, and Hungary.

(3)   *New York Times*, September 24, 1986, p. 12.

(4)   *Waterloo Courier*, April 19, 1987; Associated Press release, p. A4. Here
the Associated Press reports that Gorbachev suggested that the United States set up
separate states for blacks and other minorities. Gorbachev offered the suggestion as a
solution to U.S. race problems to a group of congressmen in mid-April, some of
whom later said they were startled by the remark. Rep. Mickey Leland (D. Texas), a
black, reportedly told Gorbachev on the way out of the meeting that the United
States doesn't handle racial relations that way. The Rev. Jesse Jackson agreed and
added that Gorbachev "would do well to focus on a solution to the treatment of
minorities within the Soviet Union as opposed to trying to focus on one he's not
acquainted with."

(5)   Freeman, R. B. and Holzer, H.J. "Young blacks and jobs: What we now
know." *The Public Interest*, 1985, pp. 18-31; Hoffman, L. W. "Work, family and the

child." In: M.S. Pallak and R.O. Perloff (eds.). *Psychology and Work. Productivity, Change and Employment.* Washington, D.C. American Psychological Association, 1986, pp. 196-220.

(6) "Native sons: Inner city black males are America's newest lost generation." *Time*, December 1, 1986, pp. 26-27; Unemployment among blacks increased 25% in 1960 to nearly 40% in 1985; see *Time*, February 2, 1987, p. 20.

(7) *Time*, December 1, 1986, op. cit.; Ellwood, David T. and Summers, Laurence. Is welfare really the problem? *The Public Interest*, Spring 1986, pp. 57-78.

(8) Otten, Alan L. Poor will find that many jobs are out of reach. *Wall Street Journal*, May 27, 1987, p. 56; also *Wall Street Journal*, June 2, 1987. This article reports that minorities presently account for nearly half the elementary and secondary population in Texas and California; projections are made concerning America's future work force.

(9) Total costs for busing at the Federal, State and local levels have never been calculated, which Mr. Nakasone would probably find incredible. In Milwaukee alone and in a single year, 30,000 staff hours were diverted into calculating the race of students to attend the various schools (Bennett, David A. *The impact of court-ordered desegregation in schools and the courts.* Eugene, Oregon: ERIC Clearinghouse on Educational Management, 1979, p. 111). More than two generations after forced busing affected every major school district of the country, William H. White the staff director for the Office of National Civil Rights Issues of the U.S. Commission on Civil Rights (USCCR) acknowledged "I'm unaware of any comprehensive study of school desegregation nationwide" (*Christian Science Monitor*, September 17, 1978). Until today, no agency has publicized an analysis of nationwide busing expenses. At a cost exceeding $300,000, the USCCR completed in 1987 a survey of how busing has altered housing patterns as a result of middle class flight (Memo from Susan Prado, Director of the USCCR, Washington, D.C., May 1987).

(10) Scott, Ralph. *Synopsis of the 1982-83 National Institute of Education Study into the relationship between desegregation and black learning.* Washington, D.C., U.S. Department of Education, 1984.

(11) *Newsweek*, June 30, 1986, p. 16; Hochschild, Jennifer L. *The New American Dilemma: Liberal Democracy and School Desegregation.* New Haven: Yale University Press, 1984, pp. 63-64; also, Wisconsin Governor Anthony Earl's actions to reduce forced busing in the Milwaukee area has been termed "racist" by Milwaukee school superintendent Lee McMurrin who insisted that busing enhanced quality education for blacks, an apparent reference to presumed achievement benefits (*Wisconsin State Journal*, April 23, 1987, p. 1).

(12) Crane, Robert L. and Strauss, Jack. School desegregation and black occupational attainment. Center for Social Organization of Schools Report. Washington, D.C.: Johns Hopkins University, July 1985, Report No. 359, pp. 1-40.

(13) Scott, Ralph *Synopsis of 1982-83 NIE Study*, 1984, op. cit.; In the Crain-Strauss study, the control sample contained more disadvantaged students, the busing was voluntary and as the project progressed increasingly large numbers of parents refused to permit their childrens' participation; the sample was not randomized, many student records were missing and far less than half the students could be located for appraisal purposes.

(14) From the 1950s until well into the 1970s it was relatively easy for civil rights leaders to convince most blacks that easy answers explained such complex issues as the black-white achievement gap. To most blacks it seemed logical that inferior black schools explained lower black learning levels. Compensatory programs such as busing seemed to make sense. No more. Too many blacks have experienced busing realities. One national poll revealed that 68% of black leaders but only 44% of blacks favor busing. After a decade of busing, 79% of Boston black parents requested the right to have children attend a neighborhood school (Wilkinson, J. Harvie III. *From Brown to Bakke: The Supreme Court and School Intervention.* New York: Oxford University Press, 1979; Also Raffel, Jeffrey A. *One Year Later:*

Parent Views Toward Schools in New Castle County after the First Year of Desegregation. Newark, Delaware: College of Urban Affairs and Public Policy, 1979; *Boston Globe,* March 5, 1982). In other cities, support for busing waned after black parents witnessed how the practice affected their children and families.

Similar trends appear concerning preferential treatment. In one poll, only 33% of blacks believed that colleges should admit some blacks whose records wouldn't normally qualify them for admission; 77% of black leaders favored job preferences compared to 23% of mainstream blacks (*Time,* February 2, 1987, p. 20).

Public opinion samplings therefore reveal what should have been apparent long ago. Blacks, like whites, want only the right to compete fairly for jobs. They want the best education for their children, whether it involves busing or neighborhood schools, colleges or a job after high school. For many blacks, educational questions are matters of special urgency. Presently about half of all teen age blacks are unemployed, in jail or unaccounted for (Milloy, Courtland of the *Washington Post.* Black unemployment: High rate among males portends a 'nightmarish' problem for society. *Waterloo Courier,* May 21, 1984, p. D1.

(15)   Illustrations describing how school personnel are urged or even coerced into diverting schools from educational functions is described in Schofield, Janet W. *Black and White in School: Trust, Tension or Tolerance.* New York: Praeger, 1982. Also, see Horstmeyer, Mark. Report: Programs for gifted students racially imbalanced. *Des Moines Register,* October 14, 1985; also, Burgess, Charles E. Harsher discipline for blacks is reported. *St. Louis Globe Democrat,* March 18, 1984; Hurwitz, Howard. Should school discipline depend on race? *Human Events,* January 24, 1981, p. 60.

(16)   Snyderman, Mark and Rothman, Stanley, Survey of expert opinion on intelligence and aptitude testing. *American Psychologist,* Vol. 42 (2), February 1987, pp. 137-144.

(17)   The potential for misuse of IQ results certainly exists and since genetic and environmental factors are interwoven they cannot be precisely parcelled out. However, statistical safeguards are commonly employed by skilled psychologists and educators; these include confidence intervals, which place the "true" IQ within a range based on test data (Sattler, J.M. *Assessment of Children's intelligence and special abilities,* Rev. ed., Boston: Allyn and Bacon, 1982).

(18)   Brookover, Wilbur B. Can we make schools effective for minority students? *Journal of Nego Education,* Vol. 54 (3), 1985, pp. 257-268.

(19)   Elliott, Rogers. *Litigating intelligence: IQ tests, special education, and social science in the courtroom.* Dover, Massachusetts: Auburn House Publishing, 1987; also, Schofield, op. cit.

(20)   Bersoff, Donald N. Regarding psychologists testily: The legal regulation of psychological assessment. In: *Psychology and the Law* (C.J. Scheirer and B. L. Hammonds, eds.) Washington, D.C.: American Psychological Association, 1983. Also, Foster, G. Susan. Court finds IQ tests racially biased for black pupils' placement. *Education Week,* February 8, 1984.

(21)   Snyderman and Rothman, op. cit.

(22)   Carpignano, Josephine. Problems in the practice of responsible school psychology. *The School Psychologist,* Division 16 American Psychological Association, Vol. 41, Paril 1987, pp. 2-4.

(23)   Cordes, Colleen. Reuben Feuerstein makes every child count. *American Psychological Association Monitor,* Vol. 15 (5), May 1984, p. 18.

(24)   Carpignano, op. cit.

(25)   Vensel, Deborah S. Assuming responsibility for the future of school psychology. *School Psychology Review,* Vol. X (2), Spring 1981, p. 182.

(26)   Mercer, Jane R. and Lewis, June F. *System of Multicultural Pluralistic Assessment: Student Assessment Manual.* New York: Psychological Corporation 1978, p. 48; Sattler (op. cit.) provides an illustration whereby the SOMPA might elevate a black child's IQ by more than 30 points (p. 280+).

(27) Exum, William H. *Paradoxes of Protest: Black Student Activism in a White University*. Philadelphia: Temple University Press, 1985, pp. 39-42. Also, see Scott, Ralph. *Mandated desegregation and black students' anomie: Historical overview of concerns expressed on the issue and summary of the empirical evidence*. Paper prepared for the Attorney General, State of Missouri, February 15, 1982.

(28) Statistically significant ethnic achievement differences are reported from the prekindergarten years through college. Scott, Ralph. Home Start: Follow-up assessment of a family-centered preschool enrichment program. *Psychology in the Schools*, April 1974, Vol. 11 (2), pp. 147-149; Scott, Ralph. Sex and race achievement profiles in a desegregated high school in the deep South. *The Mankind Quarterly*, Spring 1985, Vol. 25 (3), pp. 291-302; Robertshaw, Dianne and Wolfle, Lee. The cognitive value of two year colleges for whites and blacks. *Integrated Education*, May-December 1981, pp. 68-71; Kennedy, J. B. and Anderson, H. E. A comparative study of selected black and white (college) sophomore students in a required reading test. *Journal of Experimental Education*, 1984, Vol. 53 (1), pp. 20-28; Schofield, op. cit.; Scott, Ralph S. *Ability grouping and quality education: A review of the evidence*. Paper prepared for the Honorable W. Brevard Hand, Chief Judge of the U.S. District Court, Southern District of Alabama, October 1983.

(29) Hochschild, op. cit.; Schofield, op. cit.; *State of Georgia, et. al. Defendants — Appellees. No. 84-8771, U.S. Court of Appeals, Eleventh Circuit*, October 29, 1985.

(30) Scott, Ralph. *Ability grouping and quality education*, op. cit., 1983.

(31) Evertson, Carolyn M., Sanford J.P., and Emmer, E.T. Effects of class heterogeneity in junior high school. *American Educational Research Journal*, Summer 1981, pp. 219-232; Schofield, op. cit.; Feeney, Paul. A teacher's diary of the desegregation of South Boston High School. *South Boston Times*, Vol. 19 (26), 1986; Also, in *Birdie Mae Davis, Mobile County Alabama (Civil Action No. 3003 — 63 — H)*, the NAACP and other plaintiffs claimed that the widening dispersion of achievement scores within class was caused by desegregation. Without heterogeneous grouping, they charged, resegregation would occur within classrooms and instructional grouping of pupils.

(32) Evertson, Sanford and Emmer, op. cit.; *Birdie Mae Davis*, op. cit.; Scott, Ralph. Social class, race, seriating and Reading Readiness. *The Journal of Genetic Psychology*, 1969, 115, p. 87-96.

(33) Bilello, Suzanne. Minorities raise scores in Arlington. *Washington Star*, February 19, 1981; Scott, Ralph. Sex and race achievement profiles in a desegregated high school in the deep South, op. cit.

(34) U.S. District Judge Carr initially ordered a four year delay in implementing literacy tests in Florida. In so doing, Carr concurred with a NAACP complaint that literacy tests would deny a disproportionate number of minority students their high school certificates and that this would be unfair since, at least to a significant extent, blacks' lower achievements were associated with segregated learning (*Wall Street Journal*, December 23, 1980, p. 14; *Time*, July 30, 1979). Four years later, after blacks had attended desegregated schools, the ban on literacy tests was lifted: there were no significant pre- and post-segregation differences in the ethnic failure rates.

(35) Serow, Robert C. Effects of minimum competency testing for minority students. *Urban Review*, Vol. 16 (2), 1984, pp. 67-75.

(36) Scott, Ralph, Sex and race achievement profiles in a desegregated high school in the deep South, op. cit. Here the ethnic differences in reading averaged 3.6 grade levels, despite elevated scores which tended to artifically narrow the ethnic achievement gap. Also, see Coleman, James S., et. al., *Equality of Educational Opportunity*. Washington, D.C.: U.S. Government Printing Office, 1966.

(37) Loury, Glenn C. Why preferential admission is not enough for blacks. *The Chronicle of Higher Education*, March 25, 1987, p. 100; Simpson, Janice C. Black college students are viewed as victims of a subtle racism. *Wall Street Journal*, April 3, 1987, p. 1.

(38)   Simpson, April 3, 1987, op. cit.; Yardley, Jonathan of the *Washington Post*. Racism rears its ugly head on campus. *Waterloo Courier*, March 30, 1987.

(39)   *Time*, April 6, 1987, p. 57.

(40)   Loury, op. cit.

(41)   *Time*, April 6, 1987, p. 57; Simpson April 13, 1987, op. cit.; Another perspective is presented by Lynn Clow who notes that some whites have experienced that college black students do not want to be friends or associated with them professionally (Letter to the Editor, *Wall Street Journal*, May 6, 1987).

(42)   Simpson, April 3, 1987, op. cit.

(43)   Ibid.

(44)   To some extent the decline in black college enrollment is understandable in view of rising black dropout rates during the past two decades (*Wall Street Journal*, June 2, 1987); Also, black college enrollment is affected by such factors as the unemployment rate and infant mortality rates which are associated with physical factors which restrict learning ability (Howard, Jeff and Hammond, Ray. Rumors of inferiority. *The New Republic*, September 9, 1985, pp. 17-22. Also Howard, Jeff. Rethinking race. *The New Republic*, February 9, 1987, pp. 7-10; Pruitt, Anne S. and Paul D. "Discrimination in recruitment, admission and retention of minority graduate students. *Journal of Negro Education*, Vol. 54, 1985, p. 26+.

(45)   Unfortunately, a computer search reveals no careful investigation of possible demographic differences of black dropouts and high school graduates. Broad cultural differences appear to be the determining factors, not necessarily intelligence (Horn, Miriam. The burgeoning educational underclass. *United States News and World Report*, May 18, 1987, pp. 67-68; this is affirmed by Lavin, D.E. *Summary of the report 'Open admission at City University of New York.'* Bethesda, Maryland. ERIC Document Reproduction Service ED 097400); Lavin reports that all indices of college academic performance related more to retention than to high school grades (this may be an affirmation that "push through" policies, characterized by undeservedly high grades, is ultimately counterproductive). Further, Lavin observes that those blacks without minimum academic requirements were likely to drop out of college.

(46)   *Wall Street Journal*, June 2, 1987; national statistics indicate that 16% of American blacks score at the white average IQ (Jensen, A.K. *Bias in Mental Testing*, New York: Free Press, 1980).

(47)   Lavin, D.E., op. cit; also Bregman S.L. and Johnson, J.J. *Persistence of educational opportunity program students. Indiana University Studies in Prediction* No. 73, Bethesda, Maryland, ERIC Document Reproduction Service ED 134076.

(48)   Hawes, Chris. "Proposition 48 causes controversy" *The Northern Iowan*, University of Northern Iowa, Cedar Falls, September 23, 1986. Also, Howard, Jeff and Hammond, Ray, op. cit; Wainer, Howard. An exploratory analysis of performance on the *SAT*. *Journal of Educational Measurement*, 1984, Vol. 21 (2), pp. 81-91.

(49)   Lavin, op. cit.; since an *SAT* of 700 is below the benchmark of educable mental retardation as established by the American Association for Mental Deficiency during the pre-civil rights era and in view of the overwhelming conviction of most testing experts that the IQ is a valid and useful measure (Synderman and Rothman, op. cit) it is difficult to fault the Lavin argument that many disadvantaged students will fail if provided preferential college admisions. Separately, Dean Baker, University of Michigan regent, recently declared that "the value of a Michigan degree is in danger if the university succumbs, for whatever reason, to an admission standard which compromises academic quality." (*U.S. News and World Report*, June 8, 1987, p. 75.)

(50)   Research suggests that the average achievement scores of blacks attending college are considerably below those for whites with the same type of education (Robertshaw, Dianne and Wolfle, Lee, op. cit.); Loury (op. cit.); Also, Allen, Walter R. Black students, white campus: Structural, interpersonal and psychological correla-

tes of success. *Journal of Negro Education*, Vol. 54 (2), 1985, pp. 134-147; Allen states that black attrition rates are five to eight times those for whites on white campuses; Also, Kennedy and Anderson, op. cit. Ronald Taylor notes that only 25% of blacks enrolled at the University of California, Berkeley, graduate whereas 67% of whites get their diplomas. (*U.S. News and World Report*, June 8, 1987, pp. 75-76.)

(51) Lavin, D. E. and Silberstein, R. Student retention under open admissions at City University of New York. *Integrated Education*, Vol. 12, 1974, pp. 26-29; Tambe, Joseph T. Predicting persistence and withdrawal of open admissions students at Virginia State University. *Journal of Negro Education*, Vol. 53 (4), 1984, pp. 406-417.

(52) *U.S. News and World Report*, May 18, 1987, p. 67.

(53) *Wall Street Journal*, June 2, 1987, p. 1; Reponding to test criticisms, some colleges have announced they will discontinue requiring the *SAT*s as part of admission requirements. (*Wall Street Journal*, April 15, 1987, p. 37). If the *SAT* and similar tests are dropped, the question of test bias will remain since they correlate with achievement measures such as reading and math tests and ethnic differentials are essentially the same. If both aptitude and achievement tests are omitted as admission criteria it is difficult to understand how colleges will maintain standards so American graduates can compete with their foreign counterparts and still permit target numbers of minorities to graduate.

(54) Simpson, June 2, 1987, op. cit.

(55) Ibid.

(56) Exum, op. cit., p. 39.

(57) Allen, op. cit.; Darden, J. T. and Hargett, S. Historically black colleges and the dilemma of desegregation. *Integrated Education*, May-December 1981, pp. 48-52.

(58) Allen, op. cit.

(59) Allen, op. cit.; Exum, op. cit.

(60) *Jet* 70: 200, September 8, 1986; also, see *New York Times Magazine*. The dwindling black presence on campus, April 27, 1986, pp. 47-48; Bell, Yvonne K. and Jackson, Miranda K. Assertive behavior among black college students. *Journal of Black Psychology*, 1984, Vol. 11 (1), pp. 19-27.

(61) Fleming, Jacqueline. Chance for success better at black colleges. *Jet* 69: 24, March 17, 1986; Fleming reports that black students at white colleges achieve significantly less than at black colleges (*Wall Street Journal*, April 3, 1987, p. 1).

(62) Jencks, Christopher. Affirmative Action: Past, present and future. *Special Issue: American Behavioral Scientist*, 1985 (July-August), Vol. 28 (6), pp. 731-760.

(63) Feinberg, William E. Are affirmative action and economic growth alternative paths to racial equality? *American Sociological Review*, August 1985, Vol. 50 (4), pp. 561-571.

(64) Braddock, Jomils, Crain, Robert, McPartland, James and Dawkins, Russell. How race affects job placement decisions. *Center for Social Organization of Schools Report* No. 359. Washington, D.C.: Johns Hopkins University, July 1985, pp. 1-41.

(65) Loury, op. cit.

(66) *Time*, March 24, 1986, p. 74; Texas lawmakers, responding to political pressure, repealed portions of the 1984 school reform law that would have forced public school teachers to take tests measuring their mastery of subjects they teach. William J. Bennett, Secretary of Education, termed the action "backsliding" (*Education Week*, May 13, 1987, p. 11).

(67) Howard, Jeff and Hammond, Ray, op. cit.

(68) McKinney, G. Making the grade: Teacher testing movement threatens to screen blacks out of the profession. *Black Enterprise* 16: 24, October 1985.

(69) Griffin, J. L. Is your child a victim of education's 'dirty little secret'? (unqualified teachers). *Better Homes and Gardens*, 64: 34, October 1986.

(70) *API Readability Project: Some Interim Findings*. The Committee on Diagnostic Reading Tests, Inc. Mountain Home, North Carolina, September 28, 1982.

(71)   Howard, Jeff and Hammond, Ray, op. cit.
(72)   *New England Journal of Medicine, 1985*, Vol. 313 (15), pp. 933-952; *Journal of the National Medical Associates, 1985*, Vol. 77 (6).
(73)   Loury, op. cit.; Freeman, R. B. and Halzer, H. J., op. cit.
(74)   Milloy, Courtland, op. cit.; Also, see Wilson, William. *The Truly Disadvantaged: The Inner City, The Underclass, and Public Policy*. Chicago: University of Chicago Press, 1987. Here the author argues that race-specific policies do little to assist unskilled ghetto blacks, while aiding better prepared and more culturally advantaged blacks.

ACKNOWLEDGEMENTS

"Law and the Social Sciences: The U.S. Experiment in Enforced School Integration" originally appeared in *The Mankind Quarterly*, Summer 1982; "Playing the Social Science Card: New Option for Non-Activist Attorneys" in *The Journal of Social, Political and Economic Studies*, Summer 1985; "School Achievement and Desegregation: Is There a Linkage?" in *The Mankind Quarterly*, Fall 1983; "Sex and Race Achievement Profiles in a Desegregated High School in the Deep South" in *The Mankind Quarterly*, Spring 1985; "Mandated School Busing and Student Learning: Achievement Profiles of Third, Fifth and Tenth Grade Black and White Students" in *The Mankind Quarterly*, Fall 1986; "Desegregatory Effects in Charlotte-Mecklenburg County Schools: Longitudinal Demographics on Black Achievement and Middle Class Flight" in *The Mankind Quarterly*, Fall/Winter 1984; and ""Push-Through" Educational Programs: Threat to Academic Integrity and to the Nation's Economic Productivity" in *The Journal of Social, Political and Economic Studies*, Summer 1987.